NEW PULSE 4

Student's Book

Catherine McBeth

UNIT	VOCABULARY ▶ Getting Started	GRAMMAR ▶ Flipped Classroom
STARTER page 4	• Describing places • Present simple and present continuous • Past simple and past continuous • *used to* • Comparatives and superlatives	
1 TEAMWORK page 9	▶ Bucket lists • Skills and abilities • Life skills	▶ Present perfect with *just, yet, already, for* and *since* • Present perfect and past simple **Grammar in context:** *Slumdog Millionaire*
2 LUCKY ESCAPES page 19	▶ Disasters • Rescue and survival • Extreme adjectives	▶ Past perfect and past simple • Subject and object questions **Grammar in context:** *Touching the void*
3 YOUR FUTURE page 29	▶ Key life events • Future aspirations • Time management	▶ Future tenses • Future continuous **Grammar in context:** *England*
4 KEEP IN TOUCH page 39	▶ Forms of communication • Phrasal verbs • Non-verbal communication	▶ The zero, first, second and third conditional • Adverbs of possibility and probability **Grammar in context:** *A Midsummer Night's Dream*
5 TECHNOLOGY page 49	▶ Great innovations • Innovation and invention • Adverb review	▶ The passive • Active and passive voice **Grammar in context:** *China*
6 YOUR IDENTITY page 59	▶ Digital identity • Identity theft • Personal identity	▶ Modals of ability and possibility, obligation and prohibition • Modals of deduction **Grammar in context:** *The Invisible man*
7 THAT'S ENTERTAINMENT! page 69	▶ Entertainment • Film-making • Reporting verbs	▶ Reported speech • Reported questions **Grammar in context:** *Casino Royale*
8 PERSUADING PEOPLE page 79	▶ Adverts • Advertising • Easily confused verbs	▶ Relative pronouns • Indefinite pronouns • Reflexive pronouns **Grammar in context:** *The Pearl*
9 GET READY FOR YOUR EXAMS! page 89	▶ Exams • Vocabulary review	▶ Tense review **Grammar in context:** *Charles Dickens*
COLLABORATIVE PROJECTS	Project 1: Giving a presentation page 108 Project 2: Developing an app page 110	
EXTERNAL EXAM TRAINER: SPEAKING	Introducing yourself page 114 Talking about yourself page 116	

STUDY GUIDE page 99

READING — CULTURE BYTE	LISTENING	INTEGRATED SKILLS — SPEAKING SKETCH	WRITING
• Gerunds and Infinitives • Holiday activities: verb + noun collocations • Question tags			
• **A feature article:** *As if by Magic!* **Critical thinking:** Suggest reasons **Social awareness:** NCS (National Citizen Service) ▶ Culture Byte video	• A discussion about a life skills workshop	▶ **A youth club committee** • Speaking: An informal interview • Reading: A job advertisement	• A personal blog **Focus on language:** Adverbs of degree
• **News stories:** *Lucky escapes* **Critical thinking:** Create a timeline **Life skills:** Problem-solving (risk assessment)	• A news report about an emergency incident	▶ **A survival game** • Speaking: A group discussion • Reading: Instructions for a game	• A news report **Focus on language:** Connectors of sequence
• **Online information:** *Fantastic summer fun!* **Critical thinking:** Enquire **Social awareness:** Part-time work ▶ Culture Byte video	• A Q&A session about a foreign exchange	▶ **Work experience opportunities** • Speaking: A formal interview • Reading: Information about work experience opportunities	• A CV **Focus on language:** Writing a CV: being clear and concise
• **A profile and song:** *With a little help from his friends …* **Critical thinking:** Create **Life skills:** Effective listening	• A radio phone-in about non-verbal communication	▶ **Moral dilemmas** • Speaking: A group debate • Reading: A quiz	• Instant messages **Focus on language:** Informal expressions
• **A science article:** *STEM stars at 'The Big Bang'* **Critical thinking:** Imagine **Social awareness:** Virtual classrooms ▶ Culture Byte video	• A TV technology show about 3D printing	▶ **Great innovations** • Speaking: A presentation • Reading: A timeline	• A formal letter **Focus on language:** Writing a formal letter
• **An article and advice:** *Stolen phone, stolen life …* **Critical thinking:** Judge **Life skills:** Digital competence	• A radio discussion about ID cards	▶ **Your online identity** • Speaking: A class debate • Reading: An article	• A personal profile **Focus on language:** Connectors of cause and effect
• **A forum:** *Virtual teen forum* **Critical thinking:** Decide **Social awareness:** Entertainment and technology ▶ Culture Byte video	• Phone calls and messages about a rock festival	▶ **An entertainment survey** • Speaking: A survey • Reading: An entertainment survey	• A report **Focus on language:** Expressing statistics
• **An article with comments:** *Purrfectly persuasive …* **Critical thinking:** Categorize **Life skills:** Critical thinking	• Adverts about different products and services	▶ **Charity adverts** • Speaking: A presentation • Reading: Adverts	• A for and against essay **Focus on language:** Connectors of addition and contrast
• **A leaflet:** *How to … keep calm and pass exams!* **Critical thinking:** Summarize and evaluate information ▶ Culture Byte video		▶ **Assessment methods** • Speaking: A debate • Reading: A website	• Formal emails **Focus on language:** Formal and informal language

Project 3: Making an advert page 112

Describing photos page 118 **Collaborative task** page 120 **Discussing a topic** page 122

PRONUNCIATION LAB page 124 **IRREGULAR VERBS** page 126

STARTER
ON HOLIDAY

Vocabulary
Describing places

1 Listen and repeat the adjectives. Do they have a positive, negative or neutral meaning?

ancient   comfortable   crowded   dangerous   dirty   exciting   expensive   lively   peaceful   polluted   pretty   romantic   safe   ugly

2 Read the quiz. How many adjectives in exercise 1 can you find? Then answer the questions.

Quiz — Holiday destinations around the world

1 Spending a weekend in New York is always exciting! More than 50 million people visit the USA's biggest city every year. In which district would you find Times Square and Central Park?
- a Brooklyn
- b Manhattan

2 Come to this peaceful national park if you want to get away from it all! The Rocky Mountains span almost 5,000 km between two countries. Which countries are they?
- a Canada and the USA
- b Mexico and the USA

3 The ancient region of Cappadocia has got amazing rock formations and cave hotels. Where is it?
- a Australia
- b Turkey

4 Do you enjoy sunbathing? It's easy to find space on the sandy beach at Praia do Cassino – it isn't crowded. It's the longest beach in the world! Where is it?
- a Brazil
- b Portugal

3 Read the Look! box. Write comparative and superlative forms of the other adjectives in exercise 1.

> **LOOK!**
> **Comparatives and superlatives**
> safe – safer – the safest
> expensive – more expensive – the most expensive

4 Write sentences about places that you know. Use comparative and superlative forms of the adjectives in exercise 1.

The Turkish Riviera is more peaceful than Istanbul.
My town is the prettiest place in Mexico.

4

Grammar
Present simple and present continuous

1 Look at the table and answer the questions.

present simple
More than 70 million people **visit** Paris **every year**.
Many British people **go** abroad **once a year**.
Where **do** you **usually go** on holiday?

present continuous
We're **studying** at the moment.
I'm **not lying** on the beach **now**.
Is it **raining today**?

1 Which tense is for actions in progress?
2 Which tense is for habits and routines?
3 Which time expressions do we use with the present simple?
4 Which time expressions do we use with the present continuous?

2 Change the words in bold to make them true for you. Write one negative and one affirmative sentence for each statement.

We're visiting a museum today.
We aren't visiting a museum today.
We're learning English today.

1 We study English **six times a week**.
2 Our teacher **is telling us about her holiday** at the moment.
3 Our summer holidays start in **April**.
4 I'm wearing **a swimsuit** today.
5 My best friend lives in **New York**.
6 We're finishing **exercise 4** now.

3 Write questions using the present simple or present continuous. Then write answers that are true for you.

1 What / you / do / at the moment?
2 What time / this class / finish?
3 What / you / learn / in English / today?
4 What time / you / usually / get up?
5 Who / you / sit / next to / now?
6 How often / you / go to the beach?

Gerunds and infinitives

4 Look at the table. Match rules a–f with sentences 1–6.

We use gerunds:
a) after certain verbs (*like, love, hate, enjoy, finish, avoid, stop* …)
b) after prepositions (*in, at, for, before* …)
c) as the subject of a sentence

We use infinitives:
d) after certain verbs (*decide, want, hope, remember, afford* …)
e) after adjectives (*easy, happy* …)
f) to explain purpose

1 **Spending** a weekend in New York is exciting!
2 Do you enjoy **sunbathing**?
3 It's easy **to find** space on the beach.
4 Do you want **to get away** from it all?
5 Are you interested in **visiting** ancient sites?
6 Go to Cappadocia **to see** the rock formations.

5 Copy and complete the questions with the gerund or infinitive form of the verbs. Then write answers that are true for you. Give extra information.

Do you like … (travel)?   *travelling*
I love travelling! My favourite place is …

1 Where do you want … (go) on holiday next year?
2 Do you enjoy … (visit) quiet, peaceful places?
3 What do you usually pack before … (go) on holiday?
4 … (practise) your English, where is the best place to go on holiday?

6 Copy and complete the text with the gerund or infinitive form of the verbs in brackets.

Let's get organized!

Summer's over. Are you happy (1) … (be) back at school? Here are some tips for (2) … (get) organized:

- Use a planner (3) … (organize) your time.
- When you finish (4) … (do) your homework, remember (5) … (put) it in your school bag immediately.
- (6) … (study) effectively at home, it's important (7) … (create) a study space. Make sure it's calm so that it's easy (8) … (concentrate).
- Avoid (9) … (rush)! (10) … (get) up ten minutes earlier in the morning is a good idea.

Vocabulary
Holiday activities: verb + noun collocations

1 Word builder Read the information. Then match the verbs in A with the words in B. You can use some verbs more than once. Use your dictionary to help you.

> **COLLOCATIONS**
> A collocation is two or more words that often go together. When you learn a new collocation, write examples of other words you could use.
> hire a car / jet ski
> have a barbecue / picnic

A
get go
hire lie
swim
take visit
wear

B
abroad a bike a museum
a photo a suntan
in the sea on the beach
sightseeing snorkelling
sunburnt sun cream

2 Listen, check and repeat. 🔊 3

3 Which collocation is incorrect in each of 1–5?
1 visit **a castle** / **a picnic** / **a museum**
2 go **sightseeing** / **ice-skating** / **football**
3 hire **a bike** / **a photo** / **a car**
4 **relax** / **lie** / **swim** on the beach
5 **travel** / **get** / **go** abroad

4 Read the Look! box. Then complete questions 1–4 with *journey*, *trip*, *voyage* or *travel*. Can you answer the questions?
1 What is the quickest way to … from New York to San Francisco?
2 Where did Christopher Columbus and his crew go on their … in 1492?
3 If you take a … around the world, how many kilometres will you fly?
4 How long is the train … from London to Paris?

> **LOOK!**
> **journey (n)** = one occasion when you travel from one place to another
> **trip (n)** = the process of going somewhere and returning
> **voyage (n)** = a long journey by boat or into space
> **travel (v)** = go from one place to another, usually in a vehicle

5 Read and listen to the text about holiday nightmares. How many collocations in exercise 1 can you find? Write a list. 🔊 4

We hired bikes, …

HOLIDAY NIGHTMARES!

Home About News Comments

Annie
Our school trip to Amsterdam a few years ago was a great adventure! We hired bikes to go sightseeing round the city, went to Anne Frank's house and visited the Van Gogh museum. But while we were waiting to fly home, the airport workers went on strike so we had to get the train and ferry. We finally got home 24 hours later!

Share Reply

Jake
We used to go abroad every summer to visit my grandparents. Once, we were at the beach and we were all swimming in the sea except my dad. He was lying on the beach because he wanted to finish his book. But while he was reading, he fell asleep and got really sunburnt. Now, he always wears sun cream and stays in the shade!

Share Reply

Georgia
We had a holiday nightmare last year. On the website, our campsite looked really pretty and peaceful. But when we arrived, builders were constructing a new hotel next door. It was really noisy. Anyway, on the second day, we decided to go snorkelling. I had a special underwater camera, but while I was taking photos of all the colourful fish, a jellyfish stung me. It was so painful!

Share Reply

6 Advance your vocabulary ▶ Workbook p102

Grammar
Past simple and past continuous

1 Look at the table. Read the sentences and answer the questions.

> **past simple and past continuous**
>
> **a)** She **was taking** photos.
>
> **b)** A jellyfish **stung** her.
>
> She was taking photos **when** a jellyfish stung her. = A jellyfish stung her **while** she was taking photos.

1 Which action was longer, a) or b)?
2 Which action happened at a specific point in time?
3 Which tense do we use after *when*? Which tense do we use after *while*?

2 Copy and complete the text with the past simple or past continuous form of the verbs in brackets. Which verbs are irregular?

> My best holiday was a trip to New York last summer. While I (1) … (study) for my GCSEs, my parents (2) … (ask): 'Do you want to visit Uncle David in the USA after your exams?' Of course I (3) … (say) yes! David was living in Manhattan because he (4) … (have) a job there. I flew to JFK airport and David (5) … (wait) for me. While I (6) … (stay) there, we went sightseeing. We (7) … (visit) the Statue of Liberty and the Empire State Building. I (8) … (not spend) long in New York, but it was fantastic!

3 Write questions for the phrases in bold. Use the past simple or past continuous. Then write answers that are true for you.

I went **to Croatia** on holiday. (Where …?)
Where did you go on holiday?

1 I was **lying on the beach** last May. (What …?)
2 School started again **on 1st September**. (When …?)
3 I got up **at six o'clock**. (What time …?)
4 I was **doing my homework** at midnight last night. (What …?)

used to

4 Look at the table. Read the sentences and answer the questions.

> **used to**
>
> They **used to go** abroad every summer.
>
> They **didn't use to stay** at home.
>
> **Did** you **use to go** abroad on holiday?

1 What is the form of the verb after *used to*?
2 How does *used to* change in the negative and question forms?

> **ANALYSE**
>
> In English, we use *used to* to talk about habits in the past. How do you say *used to* in your language?

5 Copy and complete the text with the correct form of *used to* and the verbs in brackets.

> ### Holiday memories
>
> Last summer, I went to France with my parents. But when I was younger we (1) … (not go) abroad. We (2) … (stay) in a caravan in Blackpool and it (3) … (rain) all the time. I was always jealous of my friend Marie. Her family (4) … (not stay) in England. They (5) … (go) to a villa in Spain. Marie always (6) … (come) home with a suntan and stories about exotic places.
>
> Katy, 17

6 Write questions with the correct form of *used to*. Then write answers with information from the text in exercise 5.

Katy / go abroad?
Did Katy use to go abroad?
No, she didn't.

1 Katy / go to Blackpool?
2 Katy / stay in a hotel?
3 Marie / go abroad?
4 Marie / stay in a caravan?
5 Katy / get a suntan?

Comparatives and superlatives

1 Match sentences a–f with 1–6. Then write answers to the questions with your opinions.

comparatives and superlatives

a) Which is **more comfortable**, a car or a bus?
b) Which is **better**, a vacation or a 'staycation*'?
c) What is **the most popular** tourist attraction in your region?
d) Where can you eat **the best** local food in your town?
e) Which is **faster**, a train or a plane?
f) Where is **the longest** bridge in the world?

*A 'staycation' is when you stay at home for your holiday!

1 regular comparative (short adjective)
2 regular comparative (long adjective)
3 irregular comparative
4 regular superlative (short adjective)
5 regular superlative (long adjective)
6 irregular superlative

2 Look at the information. Then copy and complete the sentences with one word only.

LOOK!
= as … as
≠ not as … as
› more … than
‹ less … than

1 Florence is interesting. Venice is interesting.
   Florence is as interesting … Venice.
2 Ankara is big. Istanbul is bigger.
   Ankara is … as big as Istanbul.
3 Cádiz is ancient. Athens is more ancient.
   Athens is more ancient … Cádiz.
4 Edinburgh is expensive. London is very expensive.
   Edinburgh is … expensive than London.

LOOK!
In English we can use comparative structures with the verb *get* to show a changing situation.
Our English is getting **better and better**.
These exercises are getting **more and more difficult**.
We use …*er* and …*er* with short and irregular adjectives. We use *more and more* … with long adjectives.

Question tags

3 Look at the table and choose the correct words in rules a–c.

question tags

Question tags are small questions that we often use at the end of sentences to check information when we're speaking.
   The longest bridge in the world **is** in China, **isn't it**?

If the first verb has got a modal, we use the same modal in the question tag.
   Cars **can't** travel across it, **can they**?

If there's no auxiliary verb in the first part, we use the correct form of *do* in the question tag.
   The bridge **starts** in Shanghai, **doesn't it**?
   They **built** more than 160 km, **didn't they**?

a) If the sentence is affirmative, the question tag is **affirmative** / **negative**.
b) If the sentence is negative, the question tag is **affirmative** / **negative**.
c) We always use **names or nouns** / **subject pronouns** in question tags.

4 Copy and complete question tags. Use the auxiliary verbs in the correct affirmative or negative form, and remember to use subject pronouns.

1 The Brooklyn Bridge isn't the longest bridge in the USA, …?
2 Your sister has been to New York, …?
3 There aren't any beaches in Austria, …?
4 You can speak German, …?
5 It's your birthday soon, …?

5 Copy and complete question tags. As there are no auxiliary verbs, use the correct form of *do*.

1 Your sister went to Edinburgh last year, …?
2 It often rains in Scotland, …?
3 People don't speak Spanish in Brazil, …?
4 They dance samba there, …?
5 Your cousins lived in China, …?
6 You saw the Danyang–Kunshan Bridge, …?

TEAMWORK

UNIT 1

LEARNING OUTCOMES IN THIS UNIT
- Understand reference words in a text
- Listen for specific information in a discussion
- Practise an informal interview
- Write a blog post about a talent contest

VIDEO: GETTING STARTED
Watch the teenagers talking about skills and answer the question.

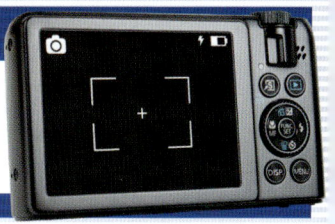

Vocabulary
Skills and abilities

1 Look at the bucket list. Listen and repeat the words in blue. Which things can you see in the photos? ♪ 5

My Summer Bucket List

1. bake cupcakes
2. catch a fish
3. design a website
4. do magic tricks
5. do something for charity
6. edit photos
7. fly a kite
8. go to a concert
9. go to a museum
10. go to the beach
11. learn a foreign language
12. learn first aid
13. learn to juggle
14. make a new friend
15. make a video blog
16. perform on stage
17. play in a band
18. read three books
19. ride a unicycle
20. run a 5K race
21. speak in public
22. watch a sunset
23. watch ten films
24. write a song
25. write computer code

2 Find words in the bucket list that mean …
1. a bicycle with a single wheel (n)
2. basic medical treatment (n)
3. to keep objects moving through the air by catching them as they fall (v)
4. to make cakes or bread in an oven (v)
5. to do something in front of an audience in order to entertain them (v)

3 Look at the verbs. Which ones are irregular? Check the past participle form of the irregular verbs on pages 126–127.

- bake
- design
- do
- edit
- learn
- make
- perform
- play
- ride
- speak
- write

do – done

4 Work in pairs. Ask and answer questions using the words in blue and *Have you ever …?* Give extra information.

💬 *Have you ever baked cupcakes?*
💬 *Yes, I have. I baked them last summer. / No, I haven't. But I've made a pizza!*

Q&A Have you ever …
1. baked cupcakes?
2. …

Vocabulary basics

9

Reading
A feature article

LEARNING OUTCOME
✔ Understand reference words

1 Read and listen to the text. Who are these people? Make two sentences for each person, using information a–g. 🔊 6

- Leah Mae Devine
- Sarah Jade
- Dynamo
- Katherine Mills

a female illusionist   *Leah Mae Devine is a female illusionist.*

a) Leah Mae's younger sister
b) an illusionist whose real name is Steven Frayne
c) a dance student
d) the first female magician to get her own show on British TV
e) a psychology graduate
f) Leah Mae's assistant
g) the star of the 'Seeing is believing' tour

2 Read the information. Who or what do the words in bold in the text refer to?

one = an illusionist

> **UNDERSTAND REFERENCE WORDS**
> Reference words refer back to people or things already mentioned, or add more information about someone or something. They are words like subject, object or possessive pronouns (*they, them, their, …*), demonstrative pronouns (*this, these, …*) or relative pronouns (*who, which, …*).

3 Read the text again and choose the correct answers.

1 Leah Mae Devine has been a magician …
   a) all her life.
   b) since she was eight.
   c) since the age of ten.

2 Leah Mae's mother …
   a) loved doing card tricks.
   b) used to do magic.
   c) wasn't interested in magic.

3 Leah Mae and Sarah Jade …
   a) are both members of the Magic Circle.
   b) have been hurt doing a trick.
   c) work together during the magic show.

4 Dynamo and Katherine Mills have both …
   a) made illusionism more popular.
   b) worked with David Blaine.
   c) written a book about magic.

DID YOU KNOW?

The Magic Circle is a British organization dedicated to promoting the art of magic. It was set up in 1905 as a 'Gentleman's club' but changed its rules in 1991 to accept membership from female magicians. There are now 1,500 members and 100 of these are female. To become a member, you have to pass a magic exam, although there is also a Young Magicians Club which is open to anyone aged 10–18.

If you've ever been amazed watching illusionists like Dynamo on television, then Leah Mae Devine is **one** to watch out for in the future.

Leah Mae has already made history by becoming the first female magician to win the prestigious 'Young Magician of the Year' competition. 'The biggest myth about magic is that "girls can't do **it**", says Leah Mae, talking to *The Independent* newspaper. **She** is now among the Magic Circle's around 7% of female members.

Just an illusion?

In recent years, illusionists like Dynamo and Katherine Mills have helped bring magic to a wider audience. Katherine Mills, a psychology graduate who was inspired by the American magician David Blaine when she was a teenager, became the first female magician to get **her** own show on British TV.

4 Words in context Find these words in the text. Match them with definitions a–f.

> assist   illusion   blade   audience
> a.k.a.   levitate

a) 'also known as'
b) to rise and float in the air as if by magic
c) to help someone
d) the sharp part of a knife
e) an appearance or effect that is different from the way things really are
f) a group of people who have come to a place to see or hear a film, performance or show

As if by magic!

Assisted by her younger sister Sarah Jade, Leah Mae has been a magician for about ten years, since the age of eight. The sisters used to watch **their** mother doing magic – **she** did more illusions than card tricks – and Leah Mae always knew that she wanted to be a magician.

So what does the future hold for Leah Mae? At the moment, she is studying dance, and a future on the stage looks likely, either as a dancer or a magician, because she has always loved performing.

And what about the trick where the magician cuts her assistant in half – does Leah Mae do **that**? Yes – but with a difference. It's Leah Mae who goes into the box and her sister **who** holds the blade. But neither of **them** has ever been hurt – not yet, anyway!

Dynamo (a.k.a. Steven Frayne) has amazed audiences worldwide with his 'Seeing is believing' tour. **He** has 'levitated' above the Shard building in London and 'walked on water' across the River Thames. Now he has just published his first book of magic secrets, so if you haven't learnt any new tricks yet, what are you waiting for?!

5 Read the information in the 'Did you know?' box. What do these numbers and dates refer to?

- 1905 • 1,500 • 10–18 • 1991 • 100

1905 = the year when the Magic Circle was set up

6 Answer the questions in your own words.

1. How did Leah Mae 'make history'?
2. Give an example of how Sarah Jade assists her sister.
3. When did Katherine Mills become interested in magic and illusions?
4. Give two examples of Dynamo's illusions.
5. What is Dynamo's book about?

7 Word builder Read the information and answer the questions.

> **SUFFIXES FOR PEOPLE**
> We add suffixes like *-(e)r*, *-or*, *-ant*, *-ist* and *-ian* to nouns or verbs to make nouns for people.
> *assist* (v) ➤ *assistant* (n)
> *illusion* (n) ➤ *illusionist* (n)

1. Find nouns for people in the text that are related to these words.

   dance   magic

2. Which suffix do we use to make the nouns for people related to these words?

   design   juggle   perform   sing   code

8 Work in pairs. Ask and answer the questions.

1. Can you do any magic tricks? If so, how did you learn?
2. Have you heard of any of these magicians before reading the text? Have you seen any of them on TV?
3. In your opinion, which trick or illusion mentioned in the text sounds the most interesting? Can you think of a logical explanation for it?

CRITICAL THINKING

SUGGEST REASONS
About 93% of Magic Circle members are male. What examples can you find in the text to show how opportunities for female magicians are changing?
Suggest reasons why only about 7% of Magic Circle members are female. Think about:
- the historical situation
- changing opportunities   • role models
- self-confidence   • ability

WEB QUEST

Work in groups of three. Find video clips of magic tricks and illusions online.

1. **Investigate** Each choose one of these illusionists. Go online and find videos of their illusions.
   • Dynamo   • Katherine Mills   • David Blaine
2. **Communicate** Share your favourite illusion with your group.

TIP! When researching people, use official websites if possible. For example, the keywords 'Dynamo official website' will take you to Dynamo's own website.

Grammar
Present perfect with *just, yet, already, for* and *since*

VIDEO: FLIPPED CLASSROOM
Watch the grammar presentation and do the task.

1 Read the sentences in the table and answer the questions.

just
We've **just** read an article about magicians. Dynamo has **just** published a book.

1 Where does *just* go in the sentence?
2 Did these actions happen recently or some time ago?
3 How do you say expressions with *just* in your language?

2 Write answers using *just* and the words in brackets.

Why are you so happy? (I / learn a new trick)
Because I've just learnt a new trick.

1 Why are you laughing?
(we / watch a funny film)
2 Why is your knee bleeding?
(I / fall off my unicycle)
3 Why does the kitchen smell so good?
(my brother / bake cupcakes)
4 Why did you turn off the TV?
(the programme / finish)
5 Why are you so pleased?
(I / finish this exercise)

3 Read the sentences in the table. Where do *yet* and *already* usually go in the sentence?

yet and already
Leah Mae has **already** joined the Magic Circle. She hasn't finished college **yet**. Have you seen her perform **yet**?

4 Look at the information and write sentences about Aisha and Ben.

Aisha has already learnt to juggle.
Ben hasn't learnt to juggle yet.

School of circus skills	Aisha	Ben
1 learn to juggle	✔	✗
2 ride a unicycle	✗	✔
3 do magic tricks	✔	✔
4 perform on stage	✗	✗

5 Read the sentences in the table. Translate answers a) and b) into your language. How do you say *for* and *since* in your language?

for, since and How long …?
How long has Leah Mae been a magician? a) She's been a magician **for** ten years. (= a duration of time) b) She's been a magician **since** she was eight. (= a point in time)

6 Write sentences with information that is true for you. Use *for* or *since* and the present perfect form of the verbs in brackets.

(be) in this classroom
I've been in this classroom for ten minutes / since ten o'clock.

1 (study) English
2 (have) this book
3 (know) my teacher
4 (be) at this school
5 (live) in this town
6 (be) a teenager

7 Write questions about the things in exercise 6. Use *How long …?* and the present perfect. In pairs, ask and answer the questions.

🗨 *How long have you studied English?*
🗨 *I've studied English for / since …*

🔍 ANALYSE

just yet already for since ever never
In English, we use the present perfect with all these time expressions. Which tenses do you use in your language?

Grammar basics   Grammar reference ▶ Workbook p84

Vocabulary and Listening
Life skills

LEARNING OUTCOME
✓ Listen for specific information in a discussion

DIGITAL VOCABULARY FLASHCARDS

Do the matching exercise to discover the new vocabulary.

active listening   assertiveness   conflict resolution   cooperation
creative thinking   entrepreneurship   money management   negotiation
problem-solving   respect for others   self-awareness   time management

1 Read the text. Which of these life skills have you used today? Listen and repeat the words in blue. ◁)) 7

What are life skills?

Life skills help us to participate in all aspects of our life successfully. Here are some different life skills:

› **SELF-AWARENESS:** understanding our own feelings and abilities
› **PROBLEM-SOLVING:** the process of finding solutions to problems
› **CREATIVE THINKING:** generating new ideas or new ways of doing things
› **TIME MANAGEMENT:** organizing our time effectively
› **COOPERATION:** when people work together
› **ACTIVE LISTENING:** the ability to listen effectively
› **NEGOTIATION:** trying to reach an agreement that everybody accepts
› **RESPECT FOR OTHERS:** treating other people with kindness and tolerance
› **CONFLICT RESOLUTION:** facilitating a peaceful end to conflict
› **ENTREPRENEURSHIP:** starting a new business or being innovative
› **ASSERTIVENESS:** the confidence to express our own opinions
› **MONEY MANAGEMENT:** being able to budget money effectively

2 **Word builder** Read the information. Then copy and complete the table with the other life skills in exercise 1. Use your dictionary to help you.

WORD FAMILIES: NOUNS AND VERBS

noun	verb
self-awareness	be self-aware
problem-solving	solve problems
creative thinking	think creatively

3 Have you ever learnt life skills at school? Which ones?

4 Look at the information below and guess the answers to questions 1–3. Then listen and check. ◁)) 8

1 Who will you hear?
2 What will they talk about?
3 Will you hear a monologue, a dialogue or a discussion?

LIFE SKILLS DAY
FRIDAY 27TH SEPTEMBER
at Newville Community School

A day of workshops to improve your life skills!
Final session (4–5pm)
In this final session we'll talk about what you've learnt, and you can give us your feedback.

Come and help us to make a vlog about your experiences!

5 Listen again. Match students 1–5 with five of the life skills in a–g.

1 Dan
2 Bella
3 Chris
4 Tessa
5 Joe

a) assertiveness
b) creative thinking
c) money management
d) time management
e) entrepreneurship
f) conflict resolution
g) active listening

6 Answer the questions. Listen again to check your answers.

1 What did Dan learn to do?
2 What do we know about Bella's character?
3 What kind of game did Chris play?
4 What are Tessa and her friends planning to do?
5 What has Joe learnt from the workshop?

Vocabulary basics   Advance your vocabulary › Workbook p103   Pronunciation › p124

Social awareness
NCS (National Citizen Service)

1 Read and listen to the text. Which of these activities are mentioned? 🔊 9

a) hiking   b) tennis   c) photography

FACT! Nearly 500,000 young people have taken part in NCS (National Citizen Service), with participants completing 12 million hours of community action.

| HOME | FIND A PROGRAMME | BLOG | FAQS | SIGN UP |

SAY 'YES' TO NCS!

NCS is a four-phase programme that gives 16-17 year olds the chance to try new things and learn new skills. The programme can improve students' CVs when planning for their future at university, college or in the world of work. This is how it works:

PHASE 1: ADVENTURE
The first part is a residential break at an outdoor centre where you can try activities like canoeing, hiking and rock climbing, as well as making new friends and challenging yourself.

PHASE 2: DISCOVERY
In the second part, you live independently in university-style accommodation (including doing your own cooking!). You can learn a new skill such as photography or drama, and develop life skills such as teamwork, assertiveness and entrepreneurship.

PHASE 3: SOCIAL ACTION
In the third part of the programme, you put your new skills into action to design a social action project. You plan, fundraise and problem-solve your ideas as a team, then go and make a difference in your local community.

PHASE 4: CELEBRATION
Finally, NCS participants celebrate their triumphs together at one great event.

I've just finished @NCS – it was the most fun I've ever had and I've made some great new friends. It took me out of my comfort zone, and I've tried so many things I'd never done before.
Emily (Hull) REPLY SHARE

I admit I had my doubts at first, but I can't believe how much @NCS has shaped me as a person! This experience has changed me so much and has helped boost my confidence and self-awareness. The best part for me was definitely the outdoor adventures.
Jess (Ramsgate) REPLY SHARE

When I was at @NCS, we raised £3,000 for a kids' charity, and I've raised even more since then. NCS opened so many doors for me and I can honestly say that it has kick-started my life!
Ollie (London) REPLY SHARE

READ MORE REVIEWS

---

2 Read the reviews again. Copy and complete the list of positive feedback.

NCS positive feedback
'It was the most fun I've ever had.'
'I've made some great new friends.'

3 Words in context Find these words and phrases in the text. What do they mean?

hiking   fundraise
out of (your) comfort zone   boost
kick-start

4 Work in pairs. Ask and answer the questions.

1. Is there a scheme like NCS for teenagers in your country?
2. Do young people do voluntary work where you live? If so, what kind of work do they do?
3. Which part of NCS would you most / least like to do? Why?

VIDEO: CULTURE BYTE
Watch the video supplied by BBC.

Grammar
Present perfect and past simple

1 Look at the sentences in the table. Then copy and complete rules a) and b) with *present perfect* or *past simple*.

past simple
When I **was** at NCS, we **raised** £3,000 for a kids' charity.

present perfect
I**'ve raised** even more since then.

a) We use the … for actions that began in the past and continue in the present.
b) We use the … for completed actions in the past.

2 Copy and complete the texts with the present perfect or past simple form of the verbs.

> I (1) … (not leave) school **yet**. I (2) … (**just** / finish) my third year. I don't know what I want to do next. **When** I (3) … (be) younger I (4) … (want) to be a maths teacher, but now I'm not sure!

> I (5) … (leave) school a few months **ago**, **last** June. In September, I (6) … (start) a catering course at college. I (7) … (be) really happy **since** I started college. I (8) … (**already** / learn) a lot of new skills, such as time management and baking cupcakes!

3 Copy and complete the table with the time expressions in exercise 2.

with the past simple	with the present perfect
ago	since

4 Write sentences which are true for you. Use the time expressions in exercise 3 and these verbs.

- finish
- live
- study
- start
- play
- have
- try

I haven't finished this exercise yet.

CLIL Grammar in context: Literature

5 Complete the text with the past simple or present perfect form of the verbs in brackets. Then listen and check. ») 10

Slumdog Millionaire
by Vikas Swarup

BOOK REVIEW

I (1) … (just / start) reading *Slumdog Millionaire*. It's about a young man called Ram Mohammad Thomas, from the slums of Mumbai. When Ram wins the Indian TV quiz show *Who Will Win a Billion?*, people think that he has cheated. How (2) … (he / know) all the answers? This book tells the story of Ram's life, from his childhood in an orphanage to his marriage to the girl that he (3) … (love) since he was 18. In each chapter, we find out how Ram knew the answers because of the experiences he had during his life.

The Indian author Vikas Swarup (4) … (write) this story in 2005. Originally the book was called *Q&A* (Questions and Answers). The book (5) … (not become) famous until the film *Slumdog Millionaire* came out a few years later.

(6) … (you / see) the film yet? I (7) … (watch) it last year and I really (8) … (enjoy) it. I (9) … (not finish) the book yet, but I would recommend it because it's a very good story.

LITERATURE TASK
Find out about the author Vikas Swarup.
1 Where was he born?
2 As well as being a writer, what job does he do?
3 Which other books has he written?

A youth club committee

LEARNING OUTCOME
✔ Have an informal interview

Today we're learning about the different roles on a committee. We're going to talk about our skills and interests, and explain why we're perfect candidates!

TASK Talk about personal skills and interests

1. Read a job advertisement
2. Understand an informal interview
3. Write answers to interview questions
4. Have an informal interview

SUNNYSIDE YOUTH CLUB
JOIN THE COMMITTEE!

- Have you ever wanted to have a bigger say in how your youth club is organized?
- Do you want to be part of a fantastic team?
- Are you well-organized, assertive and reliable?
- Then join the youth club committee!

Being on the committee is a great opportunity to initiate change and make new friends, as well as develop your own skills. It also looks good on your CV!

We're looking for the following people:

SOCIAL EVENTS ORGANIZER
Role: To organize trips, parties and events.
You need:
• Excellent interpersonal skills
• Good time management skills

SECRETARY
Role: To chair meetings and write minutes.
You need:
• Good listening skills
• Excellent organizational skills

TREASURER
Role: To assist the management with the annual budget.
You need:
• Good money management skills
• Experience of spreadsheets

WEBSITE COORDINATOR
Role: To design and update the new website.
You need:
• Code-writing and web design experience
• Photo editing skills

1 Read

1 Read the information. Which committee role involves:

1. updating the youth club website?
2. keeping minutes of committee meetings?
3. organizing a party?
4. keeping records of the finances?
5. uploading photos to the website?
6. being the chairperson at meetings?
7. using spreadsheets?
8. planning trips to the cinema or sports centre?

2 Copy and complete the sentences so they are true for you.

1. The role I would prefer is … because …
2. I wouldn't like to be the … because …

2 Listen

3 Read, watch or listen to the extract from Jack's informal interview on page 17. ◯ 11

4 Listen again and repeat. Practise your intonation.

5 Listen to the complete informal interview. Does Jack answer all the questions? ◯ 12

6 Listen again. Choose the correct answers.

1. Jack's been on the committee of his **football** / **judo** club.
2. Jack's interested in the position of **treasurer** / **social events organizer**.
3. He's good at **managing money** / **communicating with people**.
4. Jack would organize **weekly** / **monthly** trips to the cinema.
5. Kelly will phone Jack **before** / **after** the weekend.

SPEAKING SKETCH

Hi Jack! I'm just going to ask you a few questions to start with.	OK, that's fine.
Have you been on a youth club committee before?	No, I haven't. But I've had some experience of …
That sounds like good experience. Which position are you applying for?	Well, I'm really interested in the position of …
OK, so what skills do you think you could contribute?	Well, I communicate … For example, …
They're useful skills! What else makes you a good candidate for the position?	People often say that I'm …
What do you think you would enjoy most about this role?	What I find most exciting about this opportunity is …

Communication kit
- I've had some experience of …
- I'm really interested in …
- For example, …
- I'm good at … and …
- People often say that I'm …
- What I find most exciting about this opportunity is …

7 Look at the Communication kit. Which expressions are in the Speaking sketch? Watch or listen again to check your answers.

3 Write

8 Imagine you're applying for one of the roles on page 16. Prepare your interview.

> The role I'm interested in:
> My personal qualities:
> My relevant skills:
> What I would enjoy in this role:

9 Read the Communication tip. Write answers to the questions in the Speaking sketch. Use expressions from the Communication kit to give examples.

4 Communicate

10 Work in pairs. Practise your interview using the model questions and your answers in exercise 9.

> 💬 Have you been on a youth club committee before?
> 💬 No, I haven't. But I've had some experience of …

11 If possible, record your interviews. Work together to improve your style.

> **! COMMUNICATION TIP**
> **GIVE EXAMPLES**
>
> Give relevant examples of your skills and experience, so the interviewer clearly understands why you have these skills.

INTEGRATED SKILLS

Integrated skills > Resource centre

17

Writing
A personal blog

LEARNING OUTCOME
✔ Write a blog post about a talent contest

Latest posts   Photos

THE RED TRICKS
WELCOME TO OUR BLOG!

Archive   Select month < >

1 Hello! We're The Red Tricks – an indie pop band that makes pretty great music! We're Alex (on vocals), Ellie (on guitar), Matt (on guitar) and Chris (on drums). At the moment, we're preparing for the Sunnyside Youth Club Talent Contest.

2 **Getting ready for the talent contest …**   15th September, 20.45
Well, we're almost ready for the talent contest. We've practised our song a million times! We've decided to sing *Just Like Magic*. We've written a few songs since we started the band, and this one is our favourite. We haven't sung it in public yet, but we're quite confident that everyone will love it! So, the talent contest is tomorrow night … It's a bit scary, but we're up for the challenge! We're really looking forward to it …

3 **The verdict!**   16th September, 21.30
Well, the talent contest finished half an hour ago and the committee have counted all the votes. So we've just heard the amazing news – we came second! It was a really fantastic evening. We enjoyed all the performances, especially the hip-hop dance group and Kelly's juggling act. Tom's magic tricks were very funny! He deserved to win the contest. Well done, everyone!

4 Check out our new video here!
We've written some new songs – check them out here!

🔊 *Just Like Magic*   🔊 *Tricky Times*
🔊 *Media Circus*

---

1 Read the blog. Who is in the band? Did they win the talent contest?

2 Focus on content Read the blog again and match sections 1–4 with a–d.

 a) links to their material
 b) their preparations
 c) about the band / their activity
 d) the results of the talent contest

3 Focus on language Read the information. How many adverbs of degree can you find in the blog?

> **Adverbs of degree**
>
> We use adverbs of degree before adjectives to show the intensity of something.
>
> ✗   ✔   ✔✔
> not very   a bit   pretty
>   quite   very
>   really

4 Copy and complete the sentences so they are true for you.

 1 I'm quite interested in …
 2 I'm not very keen on …
 3 I'm really good at …
 4 I'd be really happy to …

5 Imagine you and your friend(s) enter a talent contest. Choose an activity and write a blog about your experience.

• sing   • play music   • do magic tricks
• do circus skills

Writing kit

1 Plan your blog. Answer these questions.
• Who is taking part?
• What are you going to perform?
• What have you done to prepare?
• Did you win the contest?

2 Write your blog. Write three paragraphs and include links to photos, video or audio.
 1 an introduction (about you / your activity)
 2 the first post (about your preparations)
 3 the second post (about the results)

3 Useful phrases

Hello! We're …   We've decided to …   Check out …
At the moment, …   We've just heard …   Well done, everyone!

4 Check your writing.

 ✔ adverbs of degree
 ✔ past time expressions
 ✔ correct past tense (past simple or present perfect)
 ✔ three paragraphs

LUCKY ESCAPES

UNIT 2

LEARNING OUTCOMES IN THIS UNIT
- Use topic sentences
- Listen for specific information in a news report
- Take part in a group discussion
- Write a news report about a survival story

VIDEO: GETTING STARTED
Watch the teenagers talking about survival stories and answer the question.

Vocabulary
Rescue and survival

1 Copy and complete the diagram with the words in the box.

capsize   casualties   catch fire
crash   firefighters   give first aid
paramedics   receive compensation
search and rescue workers
send international aid   survivors   victims

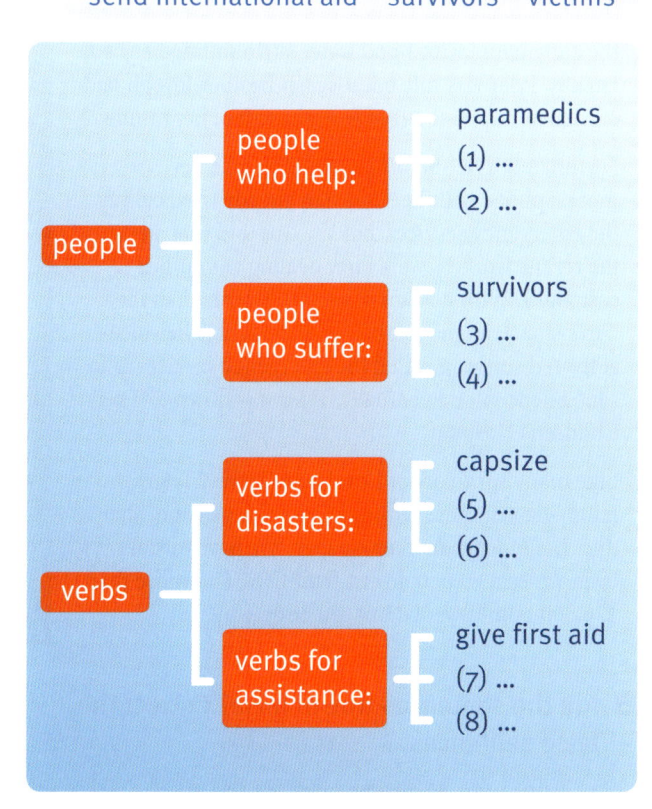

people
- people who help:
  - paramedics
  - (1) ...
  - (2) ...
- people who suffer:
  - survivors
  - (3) ...
  - (4) ...

verbs
- verbs for disasters:
  - capsize
  - (5) ...
  - (6) ...
- verbs for assistance:
  - give first aid
  - (7) ...
  - (8) ...

2 Listen, check and repeat. 🔊 13

3 Match stories 1–4 with photos a–d. Then choose the correct words.

4 Work in pairs. Would you like to do any of the jobs in exercise 1? Why (not)?

1 Firefighter dogs to retire
Toby will leave the London Fire Brigade when his handler retires. The dog has attended more than 2,000 incidents, helping (1) **paramedics / firefighters** to locate dangerous substances that might (2) **catch fire / capsize**.

2 PET SAVES OWNER
One very clever cat managed to call the emergency services the moment her owner collapsed at home. (3) **Paramedics / Rescue workers** arrived on the scene very quickly and were able to give life-saving (4) **compensation / first aid** to the casualty.

3 Ocean rescue
When his boat (5) **crashed / rescued** against rocks and (6) **caught fire / capsized**, Dimitry had a very lucky escape when a group of dolphins swam to the scene.

4 Frida: a Mexican hero
After disasters including the earthquake in Mexico City, (7) **search and rescue / casualty** dog Frida has found 12 (8) **victims / survivors** alive under collapsed buildings.

Vocabulary basics

Reading
News stories

LEARNING OUTCOME
✔ Use topic sentences

1 Look at the headlines and photos. Before reading the text, guess the correct answers.

1 These news stories are from **the USA / the UK**.
2 Both stories are about **man-made disasters / extreme weather**.

2 Read the information. Then read only the topic sentences in each news story and answer questions 1–3 about each story.

1 Who is the main character?
2 Where did the story take place?
3 What happened in the end?

> **USE TOPIC SENTENCES**
> A topic sentence is usually the first sentence in a paragraph. It gives an idea of what the paragraph is about.

3 Read and listen to both news stories and choose the correct answers. 🔊 14

1 Tyler was on the roof of her house because …
   a) she was playing there with her brothers.
   b) the hurricane had caused a flood.
   c) rescue workers told her to go there.
2 Tyler …
   a) asked Siri for help.
   b) called the helicopter herself.
   c) couldn't use her mobile phone.
3 Faith was hit by lightning while …
   a) she was driving to work.
   b) her co-workers were talking to her.
   c) she was washing up.
4 Faith …
   a) called the paramedics.
   b) was taken to hospital.
   c) suffered serious injuries.

4 Words in context Find these words in the text. Are they nouns, verbs or adjectives? What do they mean?

> flood   damage   strike   headset
>   bolt   blister

Log in | Register

Home | **News** | Sport | About

Lucky escapes

Siri saves Texan teen

Tyler Frank spent nearly two days on the roof of her house waiting for help after Hurricane Harvey had struck Houston, Texas. The 14-year-old had woken in the early hours with flood water surrounding her bed. Luckily Tyler was safe because her brother Joseph had carried her up to the roof with the rest of her family.

Fortunately Tyler hadn't forgotten to take her mobile phone with her! She had already tried calling the emergency services, but she was told that all the rescue workers were busy dealing with other casualties. With no sign of rescue, Tyler had an idea. 'Siri's smart, let me ask her!' she thought. The voice-activated software called the emergency services who sent a helicopter. Eventually, Tyler was flown to Texas Children's Hospital.

Like many survivors of Hurricane Harvey, Tyler's family have lost everything. 'Everything's gone,' she told *The Independent* newspaper. 'We have to start over.' At least 70 people lost their lives, and more than 176,000 homes were damaged or destroyed.

5 Are the sentences true or false? Correct the false sentences.

1 Tyler was 16 at the time of the hurricane.
2 Hurricane Harvey caused a lot of damage in Houston, Texas.
3 Tyler was taken to hospital by ambulance.
4 Faith worked full-time at McDonald's.
5 Faith was wearing earphones when the lightning struck.
6 The lightning went through Faith's shoe.

20 | The longer read ▶ Resource centre

DID YOU KNOW?
Worldwide, more than 2,000 people are killed by lightning every year.

Lightning strikes at McDonald's drive-thru

16-year-old student Faith Mobley from Haleyville, Alabama, had a lucky escape when she was hit by lightning at a McDonald's drive-thru.

The teenager, a part-time worker at the restaurant, had just started doing the dishes when she saw a flash of lightning outside. Before she could react, the lightning had already travelled through the building, through the washing-up water and through Faith's microphone headset, before passing through her body, down one leg, and out of her foot. When she was interviewed by reporters later, she showed them the hole in her shoe where the lightning bolt had left her body.

Faith's co-workers called the paramedics immediately and she was rushed to hospital. Dr James Hwang, who treated Faith, said she had been very lucky – lots of victims of lightning suffer more serious injuries, with clothes catching fire or the lightning causing permanent nerve damage.

By the following day, the small black blister on Faith's foot had disappeared. All that remained was the hole in her shoe and another strange phenomenon which her doctor had never witnessed before: before the lightning struck Faith had always worn glasses, but afterwards she could see perfectly well without them!

6 Answer the questions.
1 Where was Tyler when the hurricane arrived?
2 Why was her mobile phone so important in the story?
3 How much damage did Hurricane Harvey cause?
4 How did Faith feel the lightning in her body?
5 Why did Dr Hwang say that Faith had been very lucky?
6 What unusual effect did the lightning strike have on Faith?

7 Word builder Read the information and answer the questions.

UK AND US ENGLISH
Some words are different in British and American English.
smart (US) = *clever* (UK)
do the dishes (US) = *wash up* (UK)

1 Find the American English version of these phrases in the text.
   a) 'We have to start again.'
   b) a drive-through restaurant
2 How do you say these American words in British English? Use a dictionary to help you.

   cab   elevator   movie   subway
   soccer   vacation

8 Work in pairs. Answer the questions.
1 What kinds of extreme weather can cause problems where you live?
2 Have you ever had a lucky escape?
3 Do you know anyone who has been in a dangerous situation caused by extreme weather?

💡 CRITICAL THINKING

CREATE A TIMELINE
Choose one of the news stories. Identify the key events and write a list. Create a timeline of events for the story. Make sure you put them in the correct order.

WEB QUEST

Works in pairs. Find a news story related to extreme weather in your country. Prepare a news report or a video news clip.

1 **Investigate** Search online for news stories and decide which one to report on.
2 **Collaborate** Work together to create a news article or a script for your video clip.
3 **Communicate** Present your news report to the class.

TIP! Online translation tools can help you to get a general understanding of a text. Just be sure to use your own words afterwards!

Grammar
Past perfect and past simple

VIDEO: FLIPPED CLASSROOM
Watch the grammar presentation and do the task.

1 Look at the table. Choose the correct words to complete rules a) and b).

past perfect and past simple
When **the lightning struck**, **Faith had already started work**. **She hadn't finished washing up** when **the lightning went through her body**. **Had Faith always worn glasses** before **the lightning struck**?

a) After *had / hadn't*, we use the **past participle / infinitive**.
b) The **blue** actions happened **before / after** the **red** actions.

2 Read the Look! box and look at the time expressions. Which one goes between *had* and the past participle?

> **LOOK!**
> **Time expressions with the past perfect**
> Tyler had called the emergency services **before** she asked Siri for help.
> = Tyler asked Siri for help **after** she had called the emergency services.
> **By the time** the rescue helicopter arrived, Tyler had **already** been on the roof for nearly two days.

3 Copy and complete the sentences with the past simple or past perfect form of the verbs in brackets.

1 I … (hear) about Hurricane Harvey before I read this news story.
2 I … (not hear) about Tyler Frank before we read about her in class.
3 My cousins had planned to visit Texas before this disaster … (happen).
4 I … (already / do) my homework before this class started.
5 Had you heard the news before I … (tell) you?

4 Read the text and choose the correct words. Then listen and check. 15

SURVIVOR JOINS RESCUE EFFORT

When an earthquake (1) **hit / had hit** Nepal, 17-year-old Matt Moniz from Colorado, USA, was about to climb Mount Everest. He and his team (2) **already arrived / had already arrived** at base camp when an enormous avalanche suddenly (3) **crashed / had crashed** through the camp. There hadn't been any warning before the avalanche (4) **struck / had struck**, but Matt and his team were able to survive by taking cover behind a big rock. (5) **After / Before** he had survived the avalanche, Matt (6) **decided / had decided** to stay in Nepal to join the rescue operation. (7) **Already / By the time** he returned home, Matt (8) **already helped / had already helped** to build many temporary homes in the mountain villages affected by the earthquake.

5 Copy and complete the answers with the past simple or past perfect form of the verbs in brackets. Which actions happened first?

Q: Was Matt an experienced climber?
A: Yes, he (1) … (climb) other mountains with his father before he (2) … (go) to Nepal.
Q: Had he already climbed Everest?
A: No, he (3) … (not / climb) Everest before the avalanche (4) … (happen). But he returned three years later and reached the summit.
Q: Did you know anything about this avalanche before now?
A: No, I (5) … (not hear) about it before I (6) … (read) this text.

6 Copy and complete the questions with the past perfect or past simple form of the verbs in brackets. In pairs, ask and answer the questions.

1 … you … (already / study) English before you … (come) to this school?
2 … you … (already / meet) your teacher before school … (start) in September?
3 Which other English books … you … (use) before you … (have) this one?

Vocabulary and Listening
Extreme adjectives

LEARNING OUTCOME
✔ Listen for specific information in a news report

DIGITAL VOCABULARY FLASHCARDS
Do the matching exercise to discover the new vocabulary.

boiling   delighted   disgusting   exhausted   fascinating
freezing   furious   gorgeous   horrific   huge   starving
terrifying   tiny   unforgettable

1 Read headlines 1–7. Which three headlines are for positive stories? Listen and repeat the words in blue. 🔊 16

① **Exhausted** travellers return after **terrifying** helicopter crash

② Family **furious** with **disgusting** holiday accommodation

③ Jungle explorer recounts **fascinating** trip in **boiling** temperatures

④ UN sends aid as **huge** famine leaves thousands **starving**

⑤ Family **delighted** with **gorgeous** new home

⑥ **Horrific** accident caused by **freezing** weather

⑦ Top 10 **unforgettable** films made on a **tiny** budget

2 Match adjectives 1–14 with the extreme adjectives in exercise 1. Use your dictionary to help you.

1 small
2 big
3 tired
4 frightening
5 cold
6 hot
7 memorable
8 angry
9 hungry
10 beautiful
11 bad
12 interesting
13 unpleasant
14 happy

3 Word builder Read the information. Then copy and complete the sentences so they are true for you.

> **EXTREME ADJECTIVES**
> We use extreme adjectives to give emphasis.
> very bad = horrific
> We don't use normal adverbs of degree with extreme adjectives. We use *absolutely*.
> ~~very horrific~~ ✗   absolutely horrific ✔

1 The most unforgettable day I've had was …
2 It makes me absolutely furious when …
3 When I'm exhausted, I usually …
4 The most fascinating person I know is …

4 Read exercises 5 and 6. Do you think you will hear about news story a, b or c? Listen and check. 🔊 17

a) Paramedics assist accident victims
b) Teen receives compensation after disaster
c) Firefighters rescue 16-year-old from drain

5 Listen again. Choose the correct answers.

1 When she dropped her phone, Rachel was …
 a) jogging in the park.
 b) walking the dog.
 c) going to school.
2 … called the emergency services.
 a) Rachel
 b) Rachel's friend
 c) A member of the public
3 Rachel had had her phone for …
 a) two days.
 b) two weeks.
 c) two months.
4 Immediately after the incident, Rachel …
 a) received first aid from the paramedics.
 b) uploaded photos on social media.
 c) went home to have a bath.

6 Answer the questions.

1 How did Rachel try to retrieve her phone?
2 Who rescued her?
3 Was Rachel injured?
4 How long was she in the drain?
5 Could she use her phone afterwards?
6 Did Rachel mind that photos of her had gone viral on the internet?

Vocabulary basics   Advance your vocabulary ▶ Workbook p104   Pronunciation ▶ p124

Life skills
Problem-solving (risk assessment)

FACT! **Risk assessment** is an important part of problem-solving. It involves identifying the possible **risks** before you do an activity, and **taking precautions** to avoid **putting yourself or others in danger**.

1 Read the Fact box. Match definitions 1–4 with the words and expressions in bold.

1. the possibility that something dangerous might happen
2. the process of calculating how much risk is involved in a particular action
3. acting in a way that could harm yourself or others
4. doing something to protect yourself or others against possible dangers

TO THE RESCUE!
FAQS: MOUNTAIN RESCUE

What is mountain rescue?
In the UK, Mountain Rescue teams are run by trained volunteers. They work with the emergency services when people call the number 999 with mountain-related emergencies.

Who do they help?
They help anyone who's in danger in the countryside. For example, one recent rescue involved two climbers stuck in freezing conditions on the Scottish mountain Ben Nevis.

What happens when there's an emergency call?
Volunteers are on call 24/7 – that is 24 hours a day, seven days a week. When there's an emergency, they leave their normal jobs and rush to the scene.

If it's a charity, who pays for the equipment?
Mountain rescue teams operate thanks to donations. Members of the public make a huge contribution every year to pay for their operation costs.

Who volunteers for mountain rescue?
Volunteers must be over 18, physically fit, and have good navigation skills and a first aid qualification.

TOP TIP! Mountain rescue recommends that people do a risk assessment before doing any outdoor activity, to avoid putting themselves and others in danger.

Essex teen Kiera Tippett knows all about risk and rescues. She was delighted to be one of six teenagers to take part in a reality TV programme called *Hero Squad*, working next to real-life lifesavers including firefighters, lifeboat crew and mountain rescue volunteers. The unforgettable experience took them all around Britain and ended with a simulated rescue operation. Speaking to Echo News she said, 'It was such a wonderful experience and I feel very lucky to have been one of very few to train with the emergency services.'

5 STEPS: RISK ASSESSMENT
1. Identify the dangers.
2. Who do the dangers affect, and how?
3. Evaluate the risks and decide on which precautions you can take.
4. Put your precautions in place.
5. Review the assessment regularly.

2 **Words in context** Find these words in the text. What do they mean?

> run by   emergency services   stuck
> equipment   navigation

3 Read the text again and answer the questions.
1. Who do mountain rescue volunteers help?
2. What do the volunteers do in an emergency?
3. What skills and qualities do volunteers need?
4. Who is Kiera Tippett and what did she do?

4 Read the 5 steps. Have you ever done a risk assessment? In what situations would it be useful?

5 Work in pairs. Read the situation and do a risk assessment. Follow the 5 steps.

> You and some friends are planning to go hiking in the mountains next Saturday. None of you has been hiking in this area before.

Grammar
Subject and object questions

1 Look at the table. Read example questions a) and b). Translate them into your language.

subject questions

Volunteers help Mountain Rescue.
   subject   object
a) Who helps Mountain Rescue? Volunteers

object questions

Mountain Rescue helps people in danger.
    subject   object
b) Who does Mountain Rescue help?
   People in danger

ANALYSE

In English we don't use an auxiliary verb (such as *do*) in subject questions. Is there a difference between subject and object questions in your language?

2 Read the text. What does RNLI mean? How many lives has the RNLI saved since it began?

The RNLI: Saving lives at sea

The **RNLI (Royal National Lifeboat Institution)** is a charity that saves lives at sea. It helps all people who are in danger around the UK coasts, including swimmers, surfers and sailors.

The people that work for the RNLI are volunteers: there are about 4,600 crew members on the lifeboats, and thousands more that help in other ways.

The RNLI has got 237 lifeboat stations around the country and it operates 444 lifeboats. The charity has saved about 140,000 lives since it was set up in 1824.

3 Match questions 1–4 with answers a–d. There's one answer that you don't need.

1 Who does the RNLI help?
2 Who works for the RNLI?
3 What happened in 1824?
4 How many lifeboats are there now?

a) Thousands of volunteers.
b) 4,600.
c) People who are in danger at sea.
d) 444.
e) The RNLI was founded.

Grammar in context: Literature

4 Complete the text with the past simple or past perfect form of the verbs in brackets. Then listen and check. 🔊 18

Touching the Void
by Joe Simpson

I've just finished reading *Touching the Void*. It's a true story about Joe Simpson and Simon Yates, who (1) … (**climb**) the Siula Grande mountain in Peru. I (2) … (**already / hear**) about this story because there's also a film about it. I think it's one of the greatest survival stories of all time!

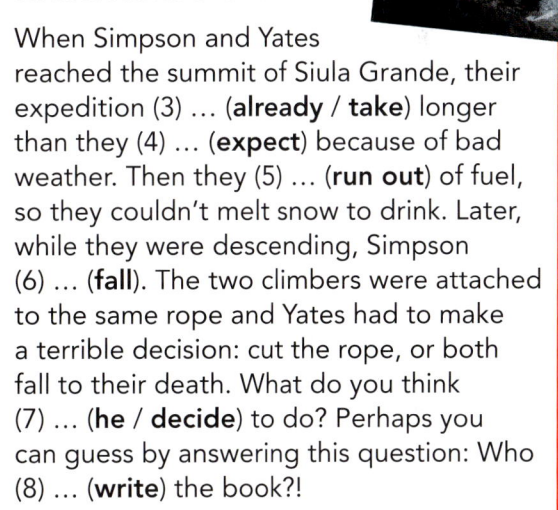

When Simpson and Yates reached the summit of Siula Grande, their expedition (3) … (**already / take**) longer than they (4) … (**expect**) because of bad weather. Then they (5) … (**run out**) of fuel, so they couldn't melt snow to drink. Later, while they were descending, Simpson (6) … (**fall**). The two climbers were attached to the same rope and Yates had to make a terrible decision: cut the rope, or both fall to their death. What do you think (7) … (**he / decide**) to do? Perhaps you can guess by answering this question: Who (8) … (**write**) the book?!

5 Read the text again. Answer the questions.

1 Which mountain had Simpson and Yates climbed?
2 Who fell?
3 Who had to make a terrible decision?
4 Who wrote the book?

LITERATURE TASK
Find out more about other survival stories. Which one is a true story?
- *Robinson Crusoe* by Daniel Defoe
- *The Hunger Games* by Suzanne Collins
- *The Odyssey* by Homer
- *I'm Bahia, the Miracle Girl* by Bahia Bakari

A survival game

LEARNING OUTCOME
✓ Take part in a group discussion

Today we're going to do a teamwork activity about survival. Which of these things do you think are the most useful?

TASK Explain the reason for your opinion

1 Read instructions for a game
2 Understand a group discussion
3 Write sentences with question tags
4 Present a group discussion

WHO WILL SURVIVE?

You and your team are going on a three-day trek in the desert.
- You each have basic food supplies, water, clothes and a map.
- Now choose five more items to take between you.
- Explain the reasons for your choices.
- How could the objects help you to survive?

- a torch
- a (1) … of matches 
- a mobile phone 
- a (2) … of cards 
- a mirror 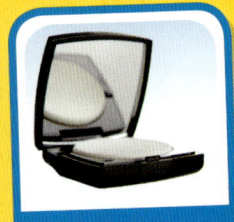
- contact lenses and a bottle of cleaning solution 
- a (3) … of gloves 
- a (4) … of sweets 
- a first aid kit 
- a (5) … of keys (with a Swiss army knife) 

1 Read

1 Read the instructions for the survival game. Complete 1–5 with these collective nouns.

- box • bunch • pack
- packet • pair

2 Work in groups. Answer the questions.
1. Who is going on the trek?
2. Where are you going?
3. How long will you be there?
4. Which five objects did you choose?
5. Which object do you think you need the most? Why?
6. Which is the least important object? Why?

2 Listen

3 Read, watch or listen to the extract from a group discussion on page 27. Why is Emily unsure about the first aid kit? 🔊 19

4 Watch or listen again. Practise your intonation.

5 Listen to the complete group discussion. Which five objects do they mention? 🔊 20

6 Match 1–4 with question tags a–d. Listen again and check your answers.

1. We'd be in the middle of nowhere,
2. That's the most important thing,
3. I don't think we'll need it,
4. It'll be boiling hot,

a) will we?
b) wouldn't we?
c) isn't it?
d) won't it?

SPEAKING SKETCH

Emily: So, what do you think the most important thing is?

Katy: Yes, and what if there was no signal? We'd be in the middle of nowhere, wouldn't we?

Jack: Well, I think we should take the first aid kit. That's the most important thing, isn't it?

Oliver: Well, I had thought that the mobile phone would be the most useful thing, but then I realized it would be useless if the battery ran out.

Oliver: Yes, I hadn't thought of that! I'm not sure if it's useful or not.

Emily: I suppose so. But it's huge! Who's going to carry it?

Communication kit
- That's the most important thing, **isn't it**?
- I don't think we'll need it, **will we**?
- It'll be boiling hot, **won't it**?
- That isn't very useful, **is it**?
- We could use that for (cooking), **couldn't we**?
- We wouldn't use that, **would we**?

7 Look at the Communication kit. Which expressions are in the Speaking sketch? Watch or listen again to check your answers.

3 Write

8 Prepare your group discussion. Write the objects in order of importance, from 1 (most important) to 10 (least important). Prepare your reasons.

1 The most important object is … because …

9 Read the Communication tip. Practise using question tags. Write sentences for your five most important objects.

We could use the mirror for making a fire, couldn't we?

4 Communicate

10 In groups, discuss your ideas. Use your notes in exercise 8 and question tags.

💬 *Who thinks we should take the first aid kit?*
💬 *I do! That would be really useful, wouldn't it?*

11 In your group, make a final decision about your five objects. Compare your choices with the other groups, and explain your reasons.

> **! COMMUNICATION TIP**
> **QUESTION TAGS**
>
> Use question tags to confirm information, check agreement or keep the discussion going.
> *That's the most important thing, isn't it?*

INTEGRATED SKILLS

Integrated skills > Resource centre

Writing
A news report

LEARNING OUTCOME
✓ Write a news report about a survival story

1 Read the news report and answer the questions.

1. Why was Sam in Australia?
2. What happened when he went for a run?
3. How did he survive?
4. What happened in the end?

WORLD NEWS

NEWS | SPORT | WEATHER | EDUCATION | MORE

SURVIVAL IN THE AUSTRALIAN OUTBACK

1 18-year-old British student Sam Woodhead was working on a farm in Australia during his gap year. One afternoon, he went out for a run, but he got lost and didn't return. He hadn't told anyone where he was going. He was missing for three days and three nights.

2 Sam had only taken a small rucksack, so he didn't have much water. It was boiling hot – over 40°C. At first, Sam drank the tiny bottle of water that he had taken. After that, he tried drinking his own urine (he had learnt this survival tip from a TV programme!). Then he found some packets of contact lens solution in his rucksack. He drank them slowly until they were finished. Finally Sam was exhausted and he thought he was going to die.

3 Eventually a search and rescue helicopter found Sam. 200 local volunteers had helped to look for him. By the time they found him, Sam was dehydrated and starving. He had lost 12 kg in three days. In the end, Sam recovered and he was delighted to survive his terrifying experience and be reunited with his family.

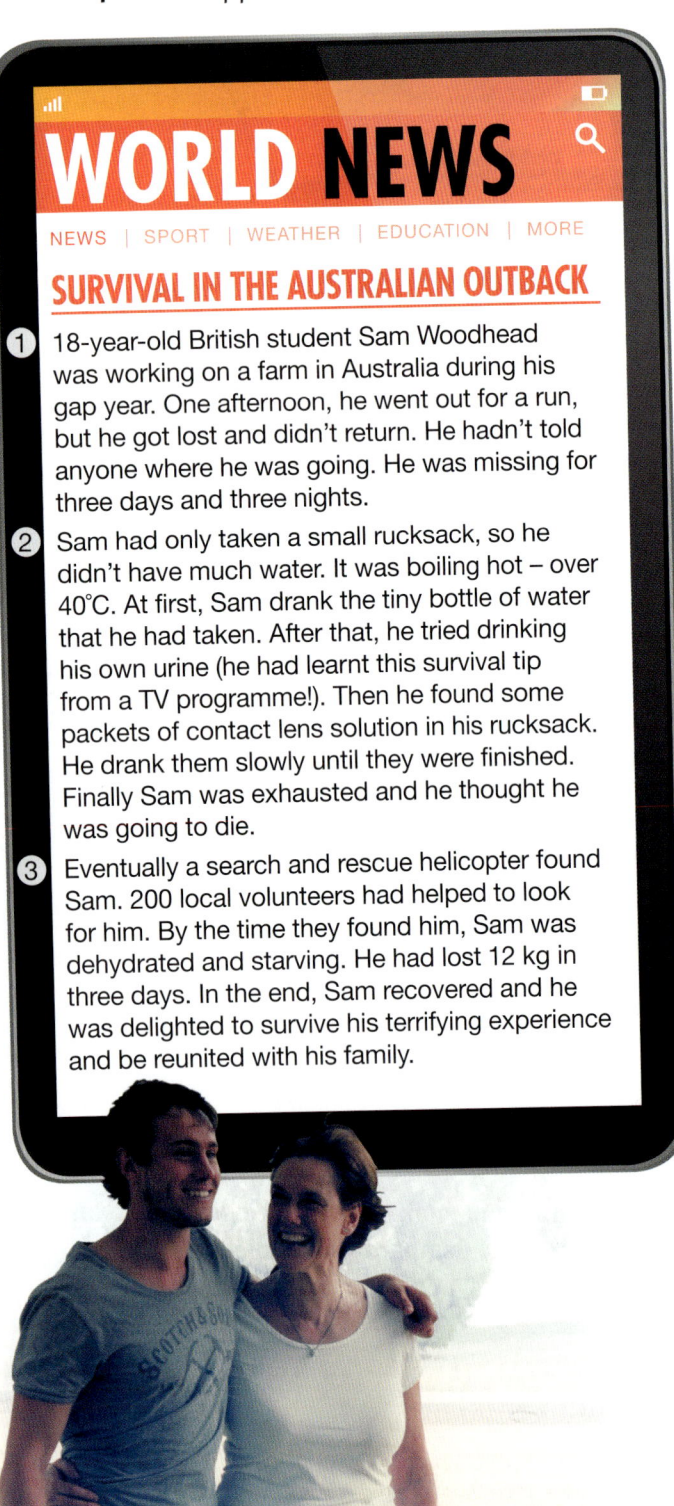

2 **Focus on content** Read the news report again and match paragraphs 1–3 with a–c.

a) narrates the sequence of events
b) explains how the story ends
c) introduces the people, place and time

3 **Focus on language** Read the information. How many of the connectors can you find in the text? How do you say them in your language?

> **Connectors of sequence**
> At first   Next   Then   Later
> After that   Finally
> Eventually   In the end

4 Choose the correct connectors.

British paraglider Guy Anderson crashed while he was flying in Idaho, USA. (1) **In the end / At first**, he tried to use his radio, but it didn't work. (2) **Next / Eventually**, he checked his mobile phone, but there was no signal. Guy had some terrible injuries, and it was very difficult to walk. (3) **Eventually / At first**, after two days, he heard a search and rescue helicopter. Amazingly, the terrifying accident didn't put Guy off paragliding, and he returned to the sky (4) **in the end / then**!

5 Write a news report about a survival story.

> ### Writing kit
>
> **1 Plan** your story. Choose or invent a story and answer these questions.
> • Who? • When? • Where? • Why?
> • What happened?
>
> **2 Write** your news report using three paragraphs:
> 1 Introduce the people, place and time.
> 2 Narrate the sequence of events.
> 3 Explain how the story ends.
>
> **3 Useful phrases**
>
> One morning / day …   After that / Then …
> At first, …   In the end, …
>
> **4 Check** your writing.
>
> ✓ connectors of sequence
> ✓ extreme adjectives
> ✓ check that you've used the past tenses correctly
> ✓ three paragraphs

YOUR FUTURE

UNIT 3

LEARNING OUTCOMES IN THIS UNIT
- Identify facts and opinions in a text
- Listen to a Q&A session and make notes
- Practise a formal interview
- Write a CV for a work experience position

VIDEO: GETTING STARTED
Watch the teenagers talking about their future plans and answer the question.

Vocabulary
Future aspirations

1. Look at the quiz. Listen and repeat the words in blue. Have you done any of these things yet?))) 21

2. Do the quiz. Do you agree with your result?

3. In pairs, compare your answers to the quiz. Which of these things do you think you will do in the future? At what age?

4. **Word builder** Read the information. Copy and complete the table with these expressions.

> arrangements   a choice   a decision
> the housework   your homework

MAKE AND DO
It's easy to confuse expressions with *make* and *do*. Check them in a dictionary and make a list in your notebook.

make	do
friends	voluntary work
money	work experience

WHAT ARE YOU GOING TO DO NEXT SUMMER?

START HERE Which of these goals is most important to you in the future?

- **Get a holiday job** and / or **make money**.
- **Get a degree** and / or learn languages.
- **Leave home** and / or travel the world.

Do you have a specific goal?

What's more important: to **pass your exams** or to **make new friends**?

Yes – you want to save up to buy a moped or **pass your driving test**.

No – you're happy to **do voluntary work**, get a part-time job or **do work experience**.

You're quite ambitious, so studying is more important.

You're a free spirit – you're ready to meet new people and explore the world!

WORK
It's definitely time to **apply for a job**. Good luck when you **go for an interview**!

STUDY
If you want to **study abroad**, you could either **go on an exchange** or sign up for a language course.

TRAVEL
The world is your oyster – it's time to **go backpacking**!

Vocabulary basics

29

Reading
Online information

LEARNING OUTCOME
✓ Identify facts and opinions

1 Read the headings quickly. What information do you think you will find out? Then read, listen and check. 🔊 22

- location • trip dates • accommodation
- price • activities • age requirements

2 Read the information. Find a–d in the texts. Are they facts or opinions?

> **IDENTIFY FACTS AND OPINIONS**
> A fact is something that can be checked and proved to be true. An opinion is based on personal beliefs or views.

a) Sharks are beautiful, gentle creatures.
b) You must already have a scuba-diving certificate before going on this camp.
c) 20% of all participants are international students.
d) If English isn't your first language, don't let that put you off.

3 **Words in context** Find these words and phrases in the text. What do they mean?

> Are you kidding?
> Don't just take our word for it!   Exactly!

4 Match the sentence beginnings and endings. Which one is *not* about Shark Camp or Space Camp?

1 Perhaps you ...
2 You'll ...
3 You'll also do ...
4 You'll be ...
5 There will ...

a) be plenty of astronaut training.
b) will find an exciting camp near you.
c) staying at the Space Academy base.
d) a marine biology project.
e) stay on Fiji's largest island.

5 Copy and complete the sentences with information from the text.

1 Some ideas for summer plans mentioned in the first paragraph are ...
2 Some parents might worry about Shark Camp because ...
3 The Shark Reef Marine Reserve is ...
4 On the final Friday at Space Camp there's ...

FANTASTIC

Home | About | **Summer camps**

What are you going to do next summer? Hopefully you won't have to stay at home and study! Maybe you're planning to go backpacking, do voluntary work or get a summer job and make some money. Or perhaps you're going to switch off and relax by the pool. But if you're thinking of setting off on a summer camp, check out these great ideas. You might not be able to go to Fiji or the USA, but perhaps you'll find something equally exciting closer to home!

Photo courtesy of Broadreach

SHARK CAMP

What is it?
A 24-day trip diving with sharks in Fiji.

Are you kidding?!
Well, it might be hard to persuade your parents to let you swim with sharks without a cage – we've all seen *Jaws*, haven't we? But apparently sharks are beautiful, gentle creatures!

OK, so where is it exactly and what else will I do?
You'll stay near the Shark Reef Marine Reserve on Fiji's largest island. You'll start off scuba diving on the reserve, and have the chance to try some white-water kayaking. You'll also do a research project about marine biology and global ecology.

Is this camp for me?
The minimum age is 15, and you must already have a scuba-diving certificate before going on this camp.

Don't just take our word for it!

> 'This trip was absolutely amazing. I loved diving with sharks, being immersed in Fijian culture and making great new friends. All in all it was an experience that I will remember for the rest of my life.'   **Sander E (17)**

SUMMER FUN!

SPACE CAMP

What is it?
A one-week camp for future astronauts.

But not in space, right?
Exactly! You won't actually travel into space – you'll be staying at the Space Academy base in Huntsville, Alabama.

And what will I do there?
There will be plenty of astronaut training, finishing off with a simulated mission to the International Space Station, the Moon or Mars. You'll also have the opportunity to fly aircraft simulators and complete team challenges such as building a space rover. The camp starts on a Sunday morning and finishes the following Friday with a special graduation ceremony.

Is this camp for me?
Advanced Space Academy is for 15–18-year-olds. About 20% of all participants are international students, so if English isn't your first language, don't let that put you off.

Don't just take our word for it!

'This experience was even more awesome than I had imagined. I'll probably never do anything so exciting again.' **Ava Ballinger**

DID YOU KNOW?
There are summer camps for learning circus skills, doing Hollywood stunts and fighting zombie battles. There's even a social enterprise camp in New York that teaches you how to get rich!

6 Word builder Read the information and answer the questions.

> **PHRASAL VERBS WITH OFF**
> One of the most common particles in phrasal verbs is *off*. Sometimes the meaning is literal, but sometimes the meaning is different.
> switch off = turn off a machine
> switch off = relax and rest

1 Find these phrasal verbs in the text. Match them with definitions a–d.

> set off   start off   finish off
> put (someone) off

   a) begin doing a particular activity
   b) begin a journey
   c) make someone not want to do something
   d) finish doing a particular activity

2 Look up these phrasal verbs in a dictionary. What do they mean?

> lift off   take off

7 Work in pairs. Ask and answer the questions.
   1 Which of these camps would you prefer? Why?
   2 Have you ever been to a summer camp?
   3 What are you planning to do next summer?

CRITICAL THINKING

ENQUIRE
Read the texts again and look at exercise 1. Identify which bits of information are missing. Write a list of questions that would help you to find out the missing information.

WEB QUEST
Find out more information about a summer camp you're interested in.

1 **Think** Choose a summer camp. It could be in your country or a different country. Write five questions about the information you want to find out.
2 **Investigate** Search online for the answers and take notes.
3 **Communicate** Share your information with a classmate, then swap. Whose summer camp sounds more interesting?

TIP! Remember to explore all areas of a website to find useful information. Click on all the different tabs or locate the site map.

Grammar
Future tenses

VIDEO: FLIPPED CLASSROOM
Watch the grammar presentation and do the task.

1 Match example sentences 1–6 with uses a–f. Do you use the same tenses to talk about the future in your language?

will / won't
1 I**'ll come** with you!
2 You **won't travel** to space.

be going to
3 What **are** you **going to do** next summer?

present continuous
4 I**'m doing** voluntary work in July.

present simple
5 The camp **starts** on Sunday.

might
6 You **might meet** people from around the world.

a) future predictions
b) spontaneous promises, offers or decisions
c) future possibilities
d) future intentions
e) schedules and timetables
f) future arrangements

2 Make spontaneous promises, offers or decisions for these situations. Use the words in brackets.

'I can't do this exercise.' (I / help)
I'll help you!

1 'It's hot in here.' (I / open the window)
2 'Is that your alarm ringing?' (I / turn it off)
3 'I'm busy at the moment.' (I / come back later)
4 'It's Jo's birthday tomorrow.' (I / bake a cake)
5 'This backpack is too heavy.' (I / carry it)

3 Write true sentences about your future. Use (*not*) *be going to* or *might* (*not*). Add more information.

live abroad
I might live abroad. Perhaps I'll move to New York!

1 stay at this school next year
2 pass my driving test when I'm 18
3 go to university
4 make a lot of money

4 Write sentences using the present simple or present continuous.

My cousins' train / arrive / at 18.10.
My cousins' train arrives at 18.10.

1 I / meet them / at the station.
2 The concert / start / at nine o'clock.
3 We / go for a pizza / before the concert.
4 What / you do / this evening?

LOOK!
be about to
I'm about to go to London.

5 Choose the correct words. Then match 1–6 with uses a–f in exercise 1.

Amy: Hi, Tom. How are you?
Tom: Fine! Hey, what (1) **are you doing** / **do you do** this weekend?
Amy: Well, I'm about to go to London!
Tom: Fantastic! What (2) **will you do** / **are you going to do** there?
Amy: I'm going to a concert with my cousins. I'm not sure, but we (3) **might go** / **are going** sightseeing, too.
Tom: Sounds great. I'm sure you (4) **'ll have** / **'re having** a fantastic time!
Amy: Sorry, Tom, I have to go. My train (5) **will leave** / **leaves** in two minutes!
Tom: Oh, OK. Have a great time!
Amy: Thanks! I (6) **call** / **'ll call** you later, OK?

6 Copy and complete the questions with the correct future tenses. In pairs, ask and answer the questions.

1 … (you / do) anything special this weekend?
2 What … (you / do) when you leave school?
3 Do you think … (you / learn) to drive?
4 … (any of your friends / be) famous one day?
5 What time … (your next class / start)?

32 | Grammar basics | Grammar reference > Workbook p88 | Pronunciation > p124

Vocabulary and Listening
Time management

LEARNING OUTCOME
✔ Listen to a Q&A session and make notes

DIGITAL VOCABULARY FLASHCARDS

Do the matching exercise to discover the new vocabulary.

develop a routine   find a balance   get organized   make a list
meet a deadline   plan ahead   prioritize   put (something) off
set a goal   set a reminder   take a break   waste time

1 Read the time management tips. Which tip do you think is most important? Listen and repeat the words in blue. ♪)) 23

HOW TO MANAGE YOUR TIME EFFECTIVELY

› Get organized! Remember to set goals, make lists and plan ahead.

› Don't waste time. Prioritize the most important things – don't put them off!

› Develop a routine for regular study and revision.

› Don't miss an important deadline! Set a reminder on your phone to help you meet a deadline.

› Find a balance between study time and free time. Don't forget to take a break every hour.

2 Copy and complete the diagram with the words and expressions in blue in exercise 1.

positive: get organized
neutral
negative: waste time

3 Copy and complete the questions with the correct verb forms in exercise 1. Then work in pairs and ask and answer the questions.

1 What goals have you … for this term in your English class?
2 How often do you … a break while you're studying? What do you do?
3 Do you ever … time while you're doing research on the internet? What are the distractions?
4 Do you ever … off doing your homework? What do you do instead?
5 Do you know how to … a reminder on your phone? Describe the process.

4 Look at the poster for a Q&A (Question and Answer) session. What will the meeting be about? Who will you hear?

Are you going on the French exchange trip?
Q&A session with Mme Blanche on Monday at 4.30 in Room 12

5 Emily is going on the exchange trip. Listen and complete her notes in your notebook. ♪)) 24

French exchange trip: itinerary

Saturday	Meet at school at (1) …
Sunday	Day with host family
Monday	Morning: At (2) …
	Afternoon: Visit to the Louvre
Tuesday	All day sightseeing, including a boat trip
Wednesday	Morning: At school
	Afternoon: (3) …
Thursday	Excursion to Versailles, travel by (4) …
Friday	Day trip to (5) …
Saturday	Return home

6 Listen again and write the following information.

1 when the deadline is for the final payment
2 the time the bus leaves on Saturday
3 the time they'll arrive in Paris
4 when the Versailles Palace was built
5 the time they'll arrive home
6 how much pocket money they might need

Social awareness
Part-time work

FACT! As of 2018, the national minimum wage in the UK is £4.20 / hour for 16–18-year-olds. It increases to £5.90 (age 18–20), £7.38 (age 21–24) and £7.83 (age 25+).

1 Read and listen to the text. Copy and complete the summary with the correct numbers. ◁)) 25

In the UK, 15–16 year-olds can work up to (1) … hours a week during school time, and up to (2) … hours a week during the school holidays. They earn the national minimum wage from the age of (3) …

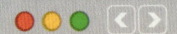

TEEN ADVICE CENTRE

HEALTH | MONEY | **WORK & STUDY** | ENTERTAINMENT | TRAVEL

Part-time work for 15–16-year-olds

Earn while you learn – and improve your future job prospects!
Part-time work is no substitute for studying, but it can be a great way to learn 'transferable' skills such as time management and dealing with customers. As long as you find a balance between schoolwork and paid work, it can even be good for your future job prospects to earn while you learn.

What hours can I work?
At age 15–16, you can work a maximum of 12 hours a week, including eight hours on Saturdays and two hours on Sundays or school days. By law, you can't work more than four hours without taking a one-hour break, and you can't work before 7am or after 7pm, or during school hours. During the holidays, you can work up to 35 hours a week.

How much will I get paid?
By law, once you're 16 you will be earning the national minimum wage.

What jobs can I do?
Due to health and safety regulations, under-16s can't do certain jobs. But sectors where companies will be looking for part-time workers include retail (shop work), catering and hospitality (for example cafés and hotels). Other options include a morning paper round, babysitting, blogging and dog walking.

Comments

Anna2000 3hrs ago
I'm 15 and I've just got a part-time job. I won't be working on school days, just four hours every Saturday. Hopefully I'll be able to find a balance with my schoolwork!

👍 Like 💬 Comment ➤ Share

EdK 25mins ago
Don't worry Anna2000 – I'm sure you'll be fine. I had a Saturday job from age 15 until I started university. Actually, I think it helps you to get organized. You learn to prioritize and plan ahead, especially when you have to meet a deadline like completing an essay. Good luck! What kind of job will you be doing?

👍 Like 💬 Comment ➤ Share

2 Words in context Find these words in the text. Match them with definitions 1–4.

> transferable skills   find a balance
> health and safety regulations   a paper round

1 the job of delivering newspapers to people's homes
2 laws that are intended to keep people safe at work
3 skills that can be used in different jobs or situations
4 do two different things successfully

3 Copy and complete the sentences with information from the text.

1 With part-time work you learn transferable skills like …
2 Under-16s can't do certain jobs in the UK because of …
3 Popular jobs for under-16s in the UK include …
4 Anna2000 will be working …
5 EdK's part-time work helped him to …

4 Work in pairs. Ask and answer the questions.

1 At what age can you legally work in your country? Is there a national minimum wage?
2 Do many young people work where you live? If so, what kind of jobs can they do?
3 In your opinion, what are the advantages and disadvantages of working at weekends or in the holidays while you're a student?

VIDEO: CULTURE BYTE
▶ Watch the video supplied by BBC.

Grammar
Future continuous

1 Look at the table. Choose choose the correct words in rules a) and b).

future continuous
Anna **will be working** four hours every Saturday. She **won't be working** on school days. What kind of job **will** she **be doing**?

a) We form the future continuous with *will* / *won't* + *be* + the *-ing* / *infinitive* form of the verb.
b) We use the future continuous for actions that will be **in progress** / **finished** at a specific time in the future.

2 Mo is going to England next week. Write sentences about what he will be doing. Use the future continuous.

1 On Friday / Mo / fly to England
2 The Smith family / wait for him / at the airport
3 On Monday morning / Mo / study English
4 On Monday evening / he / have dinner with his host family

3 Copy and complete the questions with the future continuous form of the verbs. Then write answers that are true for you.

1 What … (you / do) at three o'clock tomorrow afternoon?
2 … (your teacher / work) on Sunday morning?
3 What … (you / do) during the next holidays?
4 … (your classmates / study) this time next year?
5 Where … (you / live) in ten years' time?

4 Work in pairs, and ask and answer the questions in exercise 3.

> *What will you be doing at three o'clock tomorrow afternoon?*
>
> *I'll be having lunch. What about you?*

CLIL Grammar in context: Literature

5 Read the conversation and choose the correct words.

England
by Rachel Bladon

Amy: Hi, Mo! What are you reading?
Mo: It's a book about England. I'm getting organized for my trip!
Amy: (1) **Will you go** / **Are you going** to England?
Mo: Yes! I (2) **might** / **'m going to** study English in London.
Amy: Fantastic! (3) **Are you going to** / **Do you** stay with a family?
Mo: Yes, they (4) **'re** / **'ll be** waiting for me at the airport when I arrive.
Amy: Great! When are you going?
Mo: My plane (5) **will leave** / **leaves** on Friday morning.
Amy: Are you going to visit any interesting places while you're there?
Mo: I'm not sure yet. We (6) **might** / **'ll** visit Stratford-upon-Avon, where Shakespeare was born.
Amy: Well, have a fantastic time. And enjoy the rest of the book!
Mo: Thanks. I (7) **'ll lend** / **'ll be lending** it to you when I've finished. It tells you all about life in England. It even tells you how to make a perfect cup of tea!
Amy: That (8) **'ll** / **might** definitely be useful!

6 Listen and check your answers. 26

LITERATURE TASK

Choose an English writer from the box. Then answer the questions.

> George Eliot   Emily Brontë
> Thomas Hardy   JRR Tolkien

1 When was the writer born?
2 Where did the writer live?
3 What are their most famous works?

INTEGRATED SKILLS

Work experience opportunities

LEARNING OUTCOME
✓ Have a formal interview

> In England, most students do work experience for one or two weeks at the age of 14 or 15. Do you do work experience in your country?

TASK Prepare for a formal interview

1 Read about work experience opportunities
2 Understand a formal interview
3 Write answers to interview questions
4 Have a formal interview

WORK EXPERIENCE

This is a reminder for all Year 10 students – it's time to apply for your work experience!
Don't put it off any longer – the deadline for applications is next Friday.
Three new local employers are now offering work placements.
If you're interested in any of these, please speak to Mrs Hammond in Room 12 on Monday at 4pm.

A GREENHILLS ACTIVITY CENTRE
On this placement you'll have the opportunity to learn about the organization of the activity centre, as well as trying your hand at various sports, including canoeing, rafting, climbing and orienteering.

B THE HIGHSTREET BANK
Interested in learning about the financial sector? At the Highstreet Bank you'll be able to get hands-on experience of different areas of banking, including commercial and retail banking.

C RADIO POP FM
If you do your work experience here, you'll find out how a radio station operates, and you'll meet the production and technical staff. You'll even be able to have a go at some live broadcasting!

1 Read

1 Read the information about work experience opportunities. Which one do you think is the most interesting? When is the deadline for applications?

2 Find these expressions in the text. Then check the meaning of the phrases in your dictionary.
- try your hand at …
- get hands-on experience of …
- have a go at …

3 Write a sentence about each work placement using the expressions in exercise 2.

If you do your work experience at …, you'll be able to …

2 Listen

4 Read, watch or listen to the extracts from Emily's formal interview on page 37. When will Rachel call Emily? 🔊 27

5 Watch or listen again. Practise your intonation.

6 Listen to the complete interview. In which order do you hear these questions? 🔊 28
   a) What do you enjoy doing in your free time?
   b) What are you studying at the moment?
   c) What are you planning to do when you leave school?
   d) What are you hoping to gain from your work experience?

7 Listen again and make notes about Emily's answers to the questions in exercise 6. Then write full sentences.

   1 At the moment, Emily is studying …

SPEAKING SKETCH

The beginning of the interview ...

Hello! I'm Rachel. I work here at Radio Pop FM, and I'll be interviewing you today.	Hello! Pleased to meet you.
Please take a seat.	Thank you!
So, why are you interested in doing your work experience with us?	Well, I'm thinking about pursuing a career in the media eventually, so I think this will be great experience.

The end of the interview ...

Well, thanks for coming in today, Emily. We'll let you know our decision in a couple of days.	Great! I look forward to hearing from you.
We'll call you by the end of the week.	Thank you! It's been a pleasure to meet you.

Communication kit
- Pleased to meet you.
- Please take a seat.
- Thanks for coming in today.
- We'll let you know our decision ...
- I look forward to hearing from you.
- It's been a pleasure to meet you.

8 Look at the Communication kit. Which phrases do Rachel and Emily use in the Speaking sketch? Watch or listen again to check your answers.

3 Write

9 Choose one of the work experience placements from page 36. Explain the reasons for your choice and complete the notes.

I'm interested in this placement because ...

10 Write your own answers to the questions in exercise 6. Make sure they are about the placement you have chosen.

4 Communicate

11 In pairs, take turns to be the interviewer and practise your interviews.

💬 *Hello! I'm ...*
💬 *Hello! Pleased to meet you.*

12 Act your interview for the class. If possible, record your interviews and watch them. Do you look enthusiastic and confident?

! COMMUNICATION TIP
INTERVIEW TECHNIQUE

Remember to always be polite in an interview situation. Use formal language and shake hands. Try to look enthusiastic, calm and confident.

Writing
A CV

LEARNING OUTCOME
✔ Write a CV for a work experience position

Emily Jones

34 Market Street, Brentwood, CM5 9DL
+44 114 668120   emily.jones@email.com

Position applied for   Work experience at Radio Pop FM

Education and training   September 2017–June 2019
Currently studying for 9 GCSEs

Work experience   January 2019–present
Youth Monitor at Ultimate Fun Activity Camp

January 2017–January 2019
Volunteer DJ at Sunnyside Youth Club

Personal skills
1 …   English, Spanish and French
2 …   Excellent verbal and written skills
3 …   Excellent skills gained as secretary of Youth Club committee
4 …   Proficient with Microsoft and OS X
5 …   First Aid certificate, Guitar Grade 5

---

1 Focus on content Read the CV. Match headings a–e with sections 1–5 in 'Personal skills'.

a) Other skills
b) Communication skills
c) I.T. skills
d) Languages
e) Organizational skills

2 Read Emily's CV again. What position is she applying for? Which of her skills will be useful?

3 Focus on language Read the information. Why must you organize information clearly in a CV?

Writing a CV: being clear and concise

Employers will probably spend less than one minute looking at your CV, so you need to make a good impression quickly! Use headings and bullet points instead of full sentences.
I speak Spanish and French. ✗
Languages: Spanish and French ✔

4 Write your CV. Imagine you're applying for one of the work experience positions on page 36.

Writing kit

1 **Plan** your CV. Use Emily's CV to help you.

2 **Write** your CV. Adapt it specifically for the position you're applying for.

3 **Useful phrases**

Work experience at …   Excellent … skills gained as …
Currently studying for …   Proficient with …

4 **Check** your writing.

✔ check your spelling
✔ check all dates and numbers
✔ check you've completed all the sections

KEEP IN TOUCH

UNIT 4

LEARNING OUTCOMES IN THIS UNIT
- Take notes and summarize a text
- Listen for specific information in a radio phone-in
- Take part in a group debate
- Write an instant message conversation

VIDEO: GETTING STARTED
Watch the teenagers talking about communication and answer the question.

Vocabulary
Phrasal verbs

1 Listen and repeat the phrasal verbs in blue. Which ones are related to family life? Which ones are only used to talk about relationships? 🔊 29

2 Word builder Read the information. Which of the phrasal verbs in exercise 1 are separable? Use a dictionary to find example sentences.

> **SEPARABLE AND INSEPARABLE PHRASAL VERBS**
> A phrasal verb consists of a verb and a particle. You can separate the verb and the particle in some phrasal verbs, but in others you can't.
> Our teacher never **tells off** us. ✗
> She never **tells** us **off**. ✓
> My brother's great! I **get on** him with. ✗
> I **get on with** him. ✓

3 Copy and complete the questions with the correct particles.

FAMILY, FRIENDS AND RELATIONSHIPS

1. Who do you get … best with in your family?
2. Do your parents ever tell you …? Why?
3. Do you ever have to look … your brothers or sisters?
4. Have you ever fallen … with a friend? Why?
5. Where do you usually hang … with your friends?
6. In your opinion, what is the best age to settle …?

4 Work in pairs. Ask and answer the questions in exercise 3.

> 💬 *Who do you get on best with in your family?*
> 💬 *I get on really well with my sister. We're twins!*

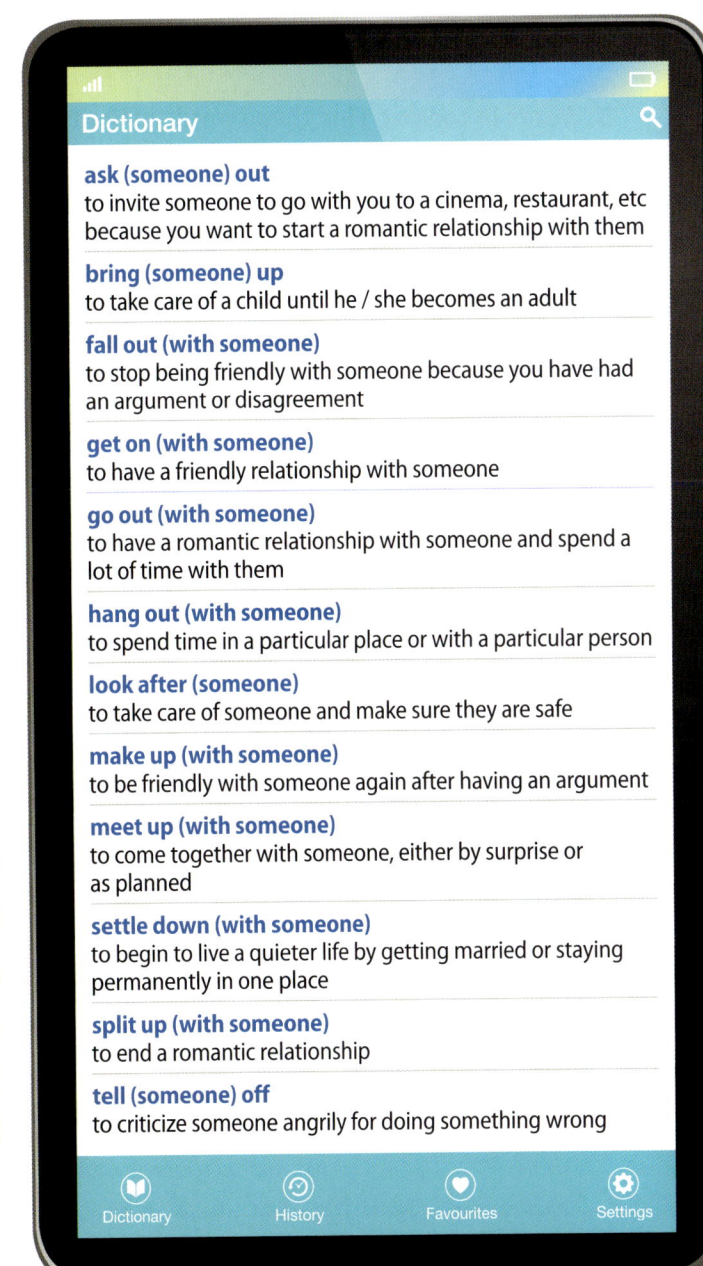

Dictionary

ask (someone) out
to invite someone to go with you to a cinema, restaurant, etc because you want to start a romantic relationship with them

bring (someone) up
to take care of a child until he / she becomes an adult

fall out (with someone)
to stop being friendly with someone because you have had an argument or disagreement

get on (with someone)
to have a friendly relationship with someone

go out (with someone)
to have a romantic relationship with someone and spend a lot of time with them

hang out (with someone)
to spend time in a particular place or with a particular person

look after (someone)
to take care of someone and make sure they are safe

make up (with someone)
to be friendly with someone again after having an argument

meet up (with someone)
to come together with someone, either by surprise or as planned

settle down (with someone)
to begin to live a quieter life by getting married or staying permanently in one place

split up (with someone)
to end a romantic relationship

tell (someone) off
to criticize someone angrily for doing something wrong

Dictionary | History | Favourites | Settings

Vocabulary basics

39

Reading
A profile and song

LEARNING OUTCOME
✔ Take notes and summarize a text

1. Look at the title. What do you think 'With a little help from his friends' refers to? Read and listen to the text and check your answer. 🔊 30

2. Copy and complete the sentences with information from the text.
   1. Isaiah Acosta is from …
   2. Isaiah collaborated with …
   3. Their first song was called …
   4. Isaiah communicates by …
   5. Isaiah loves …

3. **Words in context** Find these words in the text. Which one is a phrasal verb? Match them with definitions a–d.

   > live with   ambassador   go viral   jaw

   a) to become very popular and spread quickly on the internet
   b) someone who represents an organization
   c) to accept something difficult that you can't change
   d) the lower part of the face that includes the chin and teeth

4. Read the information. When would you need to take notes from a text?

   > **TAKE NOTES AND SUMMARIZE**
   > Decide which information in the text is more important. Think about what you'd want to include if you had to write a summary. Don't write full sentences in your notes. Use abbreviations for long words, and initials for names.

5. Put notes a–d in order. Then write a summary. What other information could you include?

   > Notes: Isaiah Acosta
   > a) produced song Oxygen to Fly together
   > b) IA (17) – can't speak but writes rap songs
   > c) also made short film and music video
   > d) worked with rapper TH

WITH A LITTLE HELP

18-year-old Isaiah Acosta was born with a condition called 'situs inversus', which has left him unable to speak. But that hasn't stopped him becoming a rap artist! With the collaboration of rapper Trap House, Isaiah released his first song, *Oxygen to Fly*, about the difficulties of living with his medical condition.

Writing is Isaiah's lifeline – his lyrics contain everything that he would say if he could speak. Over the years he has written a lot of poems, often about things that worry him. He usually composes poems on his mobile, and he communicates with others by instant messaging. Isaiah finds that rap music is the perfect way to express his feelings. It has given him a voice, and now – with the help of Trap House – he hopes to reach others whose voices are not heard.

The rapper Trap House, who was also brought up in Phoenix, agreed to be Isaiah's voice. He was very impressed by Isaiah's lyrics and creative ideas, and was delighted to work with him to transform his poem into a rap song.

So how did the rap duo get together? It probably wouldn't have happened if Isaiah hadn't been an ambassador for the Children's Miracle Network Hospitals (CMN Hospitals*). To cut

OXYGEN TO FLY
BY ISAIAH ACOSTA

I don't care what people think of me
Proud and honoured that they carry me
Jaw gone but I love myself, like a lion to my family
Heart big through a tragedy
I don't care what the people say
I don't ever say can't or won't
Had a dream to rap the other day
Just accept me for my differences
Everybody gonna hear my voice …

You can download the song if you visit your favourite music streaming service

6. Answer the questions.
   1. What is Isaiah's song about?
   2. What does the writer mean by 'writing is Isaiah's lifeline'?
   3. How do you think Isaiah's song might help others?
   4. Do you think Isaiah and Trap House became friends?
   5. What are the connections between Isaiah and the Children's Miracle Network Hospitals?
   6. Give examples of Isaiah's ability to overcome adversity.

FROM HIS FRIENDS ...

a long story short, when Isaiah expressed interest in becoming a rapper, CMN Hospitals put him in touch with Trap House. The pair got on really well when they met up and the result was not only the musical collaboration but also a short film (by director Torben Bernhard) about a music video that went viral on YouTube.

By sharing their experiences online, the rap duo has vshown the world the importance of supporting children's hospitals like CMN Hospitals.

If you watch the film, you'll soon see Isaiah's ability to overcome adversity. When doctors offered him cosmetic surgery, Isaiah turned it down – he said that he wouldn't need it unless it helped him to breathe or speak. All Isaiah wants is for others to accept him as he is – a teenager who loves music, fashion and hanging out with his friends – and to be able to give a voice to the voiceless. As they say, actions speak louder than words!

Children's Miracle Network Hospitals

* CMNH is a non-profit organisation that raises funds for 170 children's hospitals across North America, including Phoenix Children's hospital where Isaiah still receives care.

7 Word builder Read the information and answer the questions.

IDIOMS
An idiom is an expression whose meaning is different from the meaning of the individual words.
 a dream come true
 to cut a long story short

1 Find the example idioms in the text. What do they mean?
2 Find an idiom in the text that means 'what you do is more significant than what you say'. Do you have a similar expression in your language? Do you think it is true?

8 Work in pairs to ask and answer the questions.

1 Do you …
   a) listen to rap music?
   b) write poems or songs?
2 Have you ever collaborated with friends on a creative project?
3 How have your friends and / or family helped you with challenges in your life?

💡 CRITICAL THINKING

CREATE
Discuss the lyrics to Isaiah Acosta's song. Think about:
- words that rhyme
- the sound of the words (the rhythm)
- the meaning of the words
- similes or metaphors

Create a verse for a new rap song or poem. Write about a subject that is important to you personally OR your reactions to Isaiah's song.

DID YOU KNOW?
'Freestyle' is when rappers improvise – they say things spontaneously and the lyrics aren't written down. In a 'freestyle battle', two or more rappers compete to create the best improvised lyrics.

WEB QUEST
Listen online to the song by Isaiah Acosta and Trap House and read the lyrics. Find out if they have recorded any other songs together.
1 **Think** Choose the search terms to find this song online.
2 **Investigate** Search online for the song and the lyrics. Find out whether Isaiah Acosta and Trap House have collaborated on other projects together.
3 **Communicate** Share your findings with the class. If possible, listen to the song together and discuss your reactions.

TIP! Be careful with spelling when you search for specific, unusual or foreign names. Don't let the autocorrect change the spelling for you!

Grammar
The zero, first, second and third conditional

VIDEO: FLIPPED CLASSROOM

▶ Watch the grammar presentation and do the task.

1 Look at the table. Then copy and complete rules a–d with *zero*, *first*, *second* or *third*.

zero conditional
If + present simple ↔ present simple
If you **visit** Spotify, you **can** download the song.

first conditional
If / Unless + present ↔ *will / won't* +
   simple   infinitive
If you **watch** the film, you**'ll see** Isaiah's strength.

second conditional
If + past simple ↔ *would(n't)* + infinitive
If you **wrote** a song, what **would** it **be** about?

third conditional
If + past perfect ↔ *would(n't)* + *have* +
           past participle
If Isaiah **hadn't met** Trap House, he **wouldn't have recorded** a song.

a) We use the … conditional when we imagine the consequences of a situation after it has happened.
b) We use the … conditional for hypothetical situations in the future.
c) We use the … conditional for possible or probable situations in the future.
d) We use the … conditional for facts or things that are generally true.

2 Read the Look! box. Then rewrite the first conditional sentences replacing *if* with *unless*.

LOOK!
unless + affirmative verb = *if* + negative verb
If I **don't do** my homework, I'll be in trouble.
Unless I do my homework, I'll be in trouble.

1 Mum will tell me off if I don't get home early.
2 I'll meet you tonight if I don't have to look after my little sister.
3 I won't finish this exercise if you don't help.
4 I won't pass my exam if I don't study.

🔍 ANALYSE
We sometimes use the second conditional to give advice.
If I were you, I'd talk to him!
How do you say this in your language?

3 Decide which part is the situation and which is the consequence. Then write second conditional sentences.

my friends / have a problem ↔ I / help them
If my friends had a problem, I would help them.

1 I / fall out with my friends ↔ I / talk to them
2 you / make new friends ↔ you / move home
3 I / visit you ↔ you / be in hospital
4 I / be happy ↔ we / be friends forever!

4 Copy and complete the third conditional sentences with the correct form of the verbs in brackets.

1 If I'd felt ill today, I … (not come) to school.
2 What would your parents have said if you … (come) home at 4am this morning?
3 We … (not use) mobile phones if we had been born in the 19th century.
4 If we had grown up in England, we … (learn) perfect English!

5 Complete the text with the correct conditional form of the verbs in brackets.

Do you want to help people with a disability to lead an active life? Then become a volunteer 'befriender'!

Young volunteer Amy is paired with Zoe, who's autistic. If Zoe was alone, it (1) … (not be) easy for her to communicate with others, but Amy helps her. 'It makes me more confident,' says Zoe. 'Amy would help me if I (2) … (have) a problem. We have fun together!'

Amy recommends the experience. 'If I hadn't become a befriender, I (3) … (not meet) so many great people,' she says. 'If you enjoy going out and meeting new people, you (4) … (love) it. You (5) … (not know) unless you try!'

6 Copy and complete the conditional questions. Then, in pairs, ask and answer the questions.

1 … (you / hang out) with your friends if you're free this weekend?
2 Would you have met any of your classmates if you … (not come) to this school?
3 If you could go anywhere for your end-of-year trip, where … (you / like) to go?

42 | Grammar basics | Grammar reference ▸ Workbook p90 | Pronunciation ▸ p124

Vocabulary and Listening
Non-verbal communication

LEARNING OUTCOME
✔ Listen for specific information in a radio phone-in

DIGITAL VOCABULARY FLASHCARDS

Do the matching exercise to discover the new vocabulary.

frown   gesticulate   give (somebody) a hug   hold hands
kiss (somebody) on the cheek   make eye contact
raise your eyebrows   roll your eyes   shake hands
shrug your shoulders   smile   stare

1 Read the 'How to ...' information. Is this advice also true in your country? Listen and repeat the words in blue. 31

How to ...
make new friends in the UK!

Do ...
- ✔ smile and be friendly.
- ✔ make eye contact, but don't stare.
- ✔ give people plenty of personal space.

Don't ...
- ✘ kiss people on the cheek if you've never met them.
- ✘ shake hands – it's too formal.
- ✘ give someone a hug or hold hands until you know them very well!
- ✘ frown or roll your eyes – it isn't very positive.
- ✘ gesticulate too much!

Remember! You can use other actions to help communicate what you mean – for example shrugging your shoulders (if you don't know something) or raising your eyebrows (if you're surprised).

2 Copy and complete the diagram with the words and expressions in blue in exercise 1.

- positive: give (someone) a hug
- it depends ...: gesticulate
- negative: frown

3 What kind of non-verbal communication would you use in these situations? Write conditional sentences.

If I went for an interview, I'd smile and shake hands.

- you go for an interview
- you meet up with friends from your country
- you have an argument with someone
- you don't know the answer to a question in class

4 Look at the information about the radio programme and answer the questions.
1. When is the programme on?
2. What is it about?

Radio Youthzone

ON NOW: Your Call

This week on Your Call, Jason West is hosting a discussion about non-verbal communication around the world. Call us now to tell us about your experiences!

🎧 LISTEN LIVE
✉ CONTACT US

5 Listen to part of the radio programme. Which five types of non-verbal communication do they mention? 32

1. smiling
2. frowning
3. kissing
4. shaking hands
5. holding hands
6. eye contact
7. posture
8. personal space

6 Listen again and answer the questions.
1. Where did Sally go on holiday?
2. What did Sally find different about greeting people in that country?
3. Why was Dan in France?
4. What did Dan notice about shaking hands in France?
5. What is Mizuki doing in Britain?
6. According to Mizuki, what is impolite in Japan?
7. Where is Bethany from?
8. What has Bethany noticed about personal space when she has been travelling?

Vocabulary basics   Advance your vocabulary ▶ Workbook p106   Pronunciation ▶ p124

Life skills
Effective listening

FACT! We usually speak at about 120–150 words per minute, but we think at about 500 words per minute. That's why we often get distracted while listening!

1 Read the Fact box and the text. What do these numbers refer to?

- 120–150
- 7
- the number one
- 60–80

The truth about listening

Did you know that only 7% of communication involves the words you actually say? The rest consists of body language (55%) and the tone, pitch and speed of your voice (38%). So in order to be an effective communicator, you definitely need to put into practice all your non-verbal communication skills! As well as helping you to negotiate better in discussions with your parents, teachers and friends, these skills will probably also serve you well in the future – good communication skills are the number one requirement among employers.

1 Face the speaker
Show that you're listening by using positive facial expressions such as nodding and smiling. You definitely shouldn't frown or roll your eyes, as these expressions show hostility and signal a lack of interest.

2 Make eye contact
A comfortable amount of eye contact will probably put the speaker more at ease – but don't stare! You should aim to make eye contact about 60–80% of the time in Western countries, but this can differ in other parts of the world.

3 Don't get distracted
Focus on what the other person is saying, not on your planned reply. Don't try to multi-task while listening, or get distracted by your emotions. Oh, and maybe it's best to put your phone on silent, too!

4 Don't interrupt
Wait until the other person finishes expressing something before you speak. When it's your turn, don't just talk about yourself, and don't give advice unless it's asked for!

5 Interact
Summarize what you've heard, and ask questions to keep the conversation going. Perhaps you'll also want to ask for clarification to check anything that you didn't understand. Keep an open mind and don't jump to conclusions!

2 Words in context Find these words and phrases in the text. What do they mean?

> tone   pitch   requirement   get distracted
> multi-task   interrupt   keep an open mind
> jump to conclusions

3 Read the text again. Then copy and complete the sentences.
1. 93% of communication consists of …
2. Good communication skills are important because …
3. Examples of positive non-verbal communication are …
4. Examples of things you shouldn't do while listening are …

4 Choose situation a or b. Prepare what you'd say to explain the situation to your friend.

a) You're in trouble with your English teacher because you haven't done your homework for two weeks.
b) You've had an argument with your parents because they won't let you go to a party.

5 Work in pairs and follow the instructions. Then swap roles. Who is the best listener?

Student A: Explain the situation (a or b in exercise 4) to your partner.
Student B: Listen to your partner. Follow the five steps in 'The truth behind listening'.

Grammar
Adverbs of possibility and probability

1 Look at examples 1–6. Then match them with rules a–c.

adverbs of possibility and probability

1. Eye contact will **probably** put the speaker at ease.
2. **Maybe** it's best to put your phone on silent.
3. These skills will **probably** also serve you well in the future.
4. You **definitely** shouldn't frown or roll your eyes.
5. **Perhaps** you'll also want to ask for clarification.
6. You'll **definitely** need to put it into practice!

a) *Maybe* and *perhaps* go at the beginning of the sentence or clause.
b) *Definitely* and *probably* go after affirmative auxiliaries (*will*, *would*, etc) and forms of *be*.
c) *Definitely* and *probably* go before negative auxiliaries (*won't*, *wouldn't*, etc) and forms of *be*.

2 Rewrite the sentences in your notebook putting the adverb in the correct place.

My friends won't listen to me! (probably)
My friends probably won't listen to me

1. Active listening isn't easy. (definitely)
2. It's harder than you think. (probably)
3. We should learn to listen at school. (maybe)
4. There wouldn't be so much conflict if everybody listened. (probably)
5. The world would be a better place. (perhaps)

3 Answer the questions so they are true for you. Use the adverb in brackets in your answer.

What would you do if your family didn't approve of your friends? (definitely)
I'd definitely try to talk to them about it.

1. Who would you talk to if you had a problem? (probably)
2. Are your friends good listeners? (maybe)
3. Are you a romantic or a practical person? (definitely)
4. What's the most romantic film you've ever seen? (perhaps)
5. Would you prefer to go to the theatre or the cinema? (probably)

CLIL Grammar in context: Literature

4 Complete the text with the correct conditional form of the verbs in brackets.

A Midsummer Night's Dream
by William Shakespeare

A Midsummer Night's Dream is a famous play by William Shakespeare. If you see it at the theatre, you (1) … (**definitely / laugh**) because it's a great comedy. It's about the themes of love, marriage and friendship.

There are two different worlds in this story: the real world and the world of fairies in the forest. Titania, the fairy queen, has fallen out with her husband Oberon. Another fairy, Puck, wants them to make up. Secretly, Puck gives Titania a magic potion so that she falls in love with the first person she sees when she wakes up. This (2) … (**not be**) a problem if the first person she saw was Oberon. But what would happen if she (3) … (**fall**) in love with the wrong person? You will have to read the story if you (4) … (**want**) to find out!

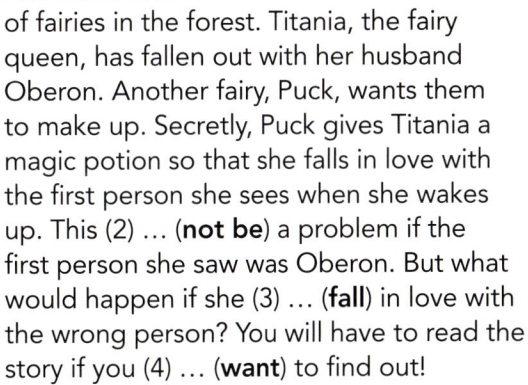

I'd definitely recommend this book – if you (5) … (**read**) it before you go to the theatre it (6) … (**help**) you to understand the play. If we hadn't studied it at school, I (7) … (**not understand**) the story because it's a bit complicated.

Oh, and did you know that if you'd been to see the play in Shakespeare's time, all the actors (8) … (**be**) men? Women weren't allowed to be actors then!

5 Then listen and check your answers. 🔊 33

LITERATURE TASK

Find out about other plays by Shakespeare. Write a short summary of one of his plays:
- a tragedy, eg *Romeo and Juliet*, *Macbeth*
- a history play, eg *Henry V*, *Richard III*

Moral dilemmas

LEARNING OUTCOME
✔ Take part in a group debate

TASK Talk about moral dilemmas

Today we're going to discuss some moral dilemmas. What would you do in these situations?

1 Read a quiz

2 Understand a group debate

3 Write sentences to present your opinion

4 Have a group debate

Quiz — Moral dilemmas: What would YOU do?

1 You've fallen out with a friend because she posted photos of you on the internet. Now, you want to talk to her about it. How would you communicate?
 a) I'd send a message – I'd rather not talk directly.
 b) I'd probably give her a ring – it would be better to talk.
 c) I'd definitely see her in person – it's hard to explain your feelings otherwise.

2 For your birthday, your boyfriend / girlfriend has given you an item of clothing which you really don't like. Would you …
 a) make an excuse and say you lost it somewhere?
 b) ask if you could change it for something else?
 c) wear it anyway, so he / she doesn't feel bad?

3 Your best friend has got a new hairstyle which you think looks terrible. When he / she asks you what you think, what would you say?
 a) I'd tell the truth. I couldn't lie to my best friend.
 b) I'd say it looks great. I'd hate to hurt his / her feelings.
 c) I'd probably keep quiet and try to change the subject.

4 Your brother has left his mobile phone in your room by accident. What would you do?
 a) Read his messages of course! Who wouldn't?
 b) Perhaps I'd use it to negotiate a favour.
 c) I wouldn't want to feel guilty, so I'd give it straight back. That's what I hope he would do for me!

1 Read

1 Read the quiz and look at Oliver's choices. Would you have chosen the same answers? Write a sentence for each question.

1 I would / wouldn't have chosen the same answer as Oliver because …

2 Match verbs from A with words from B to make expressions from the quiz. How do you say them in your language? Write example sentences.

A
• feel • give • hurt • keep • make • tell

B
• an excuse • guilty • quiet • the truth
• somebody a ring • somebody's feelings

give somebody a ring
I'll give you a ring tonight at six o'clock.

2 Listen

3 Read, watch or listen to the extract from the group debate on page 47. Who changes their mind? 🔊 34

4 Watch or listen again. Practise your intonation.

5 Listen to the next part of the group debate. Which moral dilemma are they discussing? Which four opinions do you hear? 🔊 35

 1 'I think it would be best to admit that you don't like it.'
 2 'I don't think it's a good idea to fall out about it.'
 3 'Personally, I don't think it really matters.'
 4 'In my view, you have to be assertive.'
 5 'If you ask me, it's a bad idea for a present!'
 6 'I'd say that you should change it for something else.'

Teacher: OK. Today we're going to discuss some moral dilemmas. First of all, how would you choose to communicate with a friend if you had fallen out about something? Who would like to start?

Emily: No, neither do I. If I fell out with my friend, she would probably just misinterpret my messages.

Jack: So do I. In my opinion, you can't really understand someone properly if you can't see their body language.

Oliver: Personally, I'd say that it would be best to give them a ring. I don't think that text messages are a good idea when you've fallen out with someone.

Katy: I agree. But if you ask me, I think it would be even better to talk face to face.

Oliver: Yes, perhaps you're right. I think talking face-to-face would probably be better than speaking on the phone.

Communication kit
- Personally, I'd say that ...
- I think / don't think that ...
- If you ask me, ...
- In my opinion, ...
- In my view, ...
- For me, ...

6 Look at the Communication kit. Which phrases are in the Speaking sketch? Listen again to check your answers.

3 Write

7 Prepare for a group debate about the third dilemma in the quiz on page 46. Think about the consequences of each action. Write your ideas.

8 Write sentences to present your opinions. Use your ideas in exercise 7 and the phrases in the Communication kit.

For me, the best thing to do would be ...
I don't think it's a good idea to ...

4 Communicate

9 Before the debate, work in pairs. Practise presenting your opinions, and agreeing or disagreeing with your partner.

💬 *I think that it would be best to ...*
💬 *Yes, so do I!*

10 Have a group debate about the third dilemma. Do your classmates agree or disagree?

11 Now discuss the fourth dilemma in the quiz on page 46. Can you think of any more moral dilemmas?

! COMMUNICATION TIP
USING SO, NEITHER AND TOO

Use *so*, *neither* and *too* to agree with someone.
I think it's best to tell the truth. Yes, **so** do I. / Me, **too**.
I don't think it's a good idea to lie. No, **neither** do I. / Me **neither**.

Writing
Instant messages

LEARNING OUTCOME
✔ Write an instant message conversation

1 Hi Sara, how's it going? I've got a problem with your birthday party next Saturday. My mum won't let me get the night bus home on my own. It's so frustrating! I'm old enough to look after myself!!

2 Oh no! 😣 So what time will you have to leave? I don't want you to miss the end of the party!

3 Mum said she'd pick me up at ten. That's too early IMO …

4 Yeah, you won't be able to go to the disco with us unless you can leave later! Why don't you go back with Lou? Her dad's picking her up at 12. If I were you, I'd ask them. I'm sure they'd give you a lift if you asked.

5 Yes, I hadn't thought of that. Good idea, and my mum will definitely be happier with that plan. I'll message Lou and ask her if that's OK. Thanks, Sara! TTYL 😀

6 Good luck! Bye for now!

1 Read the instant message conversation. What is Julia's problem? What solution does Sara suggest?

2 Focus on content Read the conversation again and match messages 1–6 with a–f.
- a) giving more details
- b) sharing the problem
- c) responding to the solution
- d) asking for more details
- e) saying goodbye
- f) suggesting a solution

3 Focus on language Read the information. How do you say the informal expressions in your language?

Exclamations and personal questions
Oh no!
How's it going?

Phrasal verbs and colloquial expressions
She said she'd pick me up at ten.
I'm sure they'd give you a lift.

Abbreviations
IMO = in my opinion
TTYL = talk to you later

4 How many other examples of informal language can you find in the instant message conversation?

5 Imagine you receive this message from a friend. Write an instant message conversation between you and your friend where you find a way to resolve the problem.

> Hi! How's it going? I'm afraid I've got a problem with our plan to meet up on Saturday. I've got to look after my little sister until four o'clock …

Writing kit

1 Plan your instant message conversation. What solution will you suggest to resolve the problem?

2 Write the instant message conversation. Write five parts: three from you and two more from your friend.

3 Useful phrases

How's it going?	Why don't you …?	Good luck!
Oh no!	If I were you …	

4 Check your writing.

- ✔ exclamations, abbreviations and personal questions
- ✔ phrasal verbs and colloquial expressions
- ✔ use the correct tenses in conditional sentences
- ✔ check you've suggested a solution to the problem

Study guide ▶ p102   Writing hub ▶ Workbook p118

TECHNOLOGY

UNIT 5

LEARNING OUTCOMES IN THIS UNIT
- Scan for names, numbers and abbreviations
- Understand technical instructions
- Give a presentation
- Write a formal letter of complaint

VIDEO: GETTING STARTED
Watch the teenagers talking about innovations and answer the question.

Vocabulary
Innovation and invention

1 Read the quiz and check the meaning of the words in blue. Have you seen or used any of these innovations?

2 Do the quiz. Which statements are not true?

Quiz: Fact or fiction?

1. In some parts of the USA, driverless cars already travel on public roads.

2. The future of high-speed trains is magnetic levitation! Maglev trains take people to Shanghai airport at speeds of up to 431 km/hr.

3. Smart materials are already used to make protective jackets which give attackers an electric shock.

4. 3D printing is now an affordable reality. You can buy a 3D printer for less than £200.

5. Wearable gadgets include a hat which scientists have developed to improve memory.

6. Millions of e-books have been sold since the first e-reader was designed in 2007.

7. Unlike traditional plastic, bioplastics are biodegradable. They can even be made from vegetables!

8. In desert countries such as Kuwait and Saudi Arabia people use desalinated water, which was originally sea water.

9. Flexible smartphones are much lighter, and they don't break if you drop them!

10. No wi-fi? Don't worry – now everyone can connect with satellite broadband.

11. China is building a space station in orbit, which it hopes to open by 2022.

12. How about space tourism for your next holiday? If you've got $250,000, you can sign up now!

Check your score!

3 Write the words in blue in exercise 1 under these headings. Then listen, check and repeat. ◀)) 36

communication	entertainment	the environment	manufacturing	space travel	transport

4 What is your experience of these innovations? Write sentences. Compare with your partner.

💬 *I've got a wearable gadget – it tells me how many steps I walk every day!*

Vocabulary basics

Reading
A science article

LEARNING OUTCOME
✔ Scan for names, numbers and abbreviations

1 Read the information and scan the text quickly. Find at least three names, numbers and abbreviations / acronyms. What clues do they give you about the content of the text?

> **SCAN FOR NAMES, NUMBERS AND ABBREVIATIONS**
> Names, numbers and abbreviations stand out when you look at a text. If you scan them quickly, you can get some good clues to what the text is about.

2 Read and listen to the text. Choose the best summary, a or b. 🔊 37

The article is about …
a) science fairs for young people in the EU and USA, and how previous winners have developed their STEM / STEAM careers.
b) the annual 'Big Bang' STEM fair in Britain, including information about recent winners, the selection process, and the stands and events at last year's fair.

3 Copy and complete the sentences with names, numbers and abbreviations / acronyms from the text.

1 Britain's biggest STEM fair for young people is called …
2 The two top winners at the recent fair were …
3 … visitors attended the fair last year.
4 The fair was held at the …
5 The name of the nanotechnology exhibition was …

4 **Words in context** Find these words in the text. Are they nouns or verbs? Match them with definitions a–e.

> award   fair   stand   nanotechnology   pitch

a) the construction and use of very small structures, using atoms and molecules
b) a prize that is given to someone who has achieved something
c) an event where people or companies bring their products for you to look at
d) to try to sell something by saying how good it is
e) a table at an exhibition where people show or sell information, products or services

STEM* stars at 'The Big Bang'

Meet Josh Mitchell and Emily Xu, winners of this year's UK Young Engineer and GSK UK Young Scientist of the Year awards at The Big Bang Fair, the UK's biggest STEM fair for young people.

Emily Xu

Young engineer Josh was awarded the top prize for his project to design an inexpensive 3D printer. The flat-pack machine, called 'The Plybot', fits into two 13-inch pizza boxes and can be assembled very easily. If Josh can market his product, it will be sold for just £49. Meanwhile, Emily won the top science prize for her project to create safer and more effective pharmaceutical drugs.

The Big Bang UK Young Scientists & Engineers Fair is held every year to celebrate achievements and inspire young people in STEM. More than 80,000 visitors attended last year's fair, which was held at the National Exhibition Centre (NEC) in Birmingham. As well as interactive exhibitions and careers talks, there were also more than 150 stands about everything from bioplastics and satellite broadband

Josh Mitchell

5 Are the sentences true or false? Correct the false sentences.

1 Josh Mitchell designed a flexible phone.
2 Emily Xu won the top prize for engineering.
3 The Big Bang fair is held every year.
4 500 finalists are selected from around the world.
5 You can enter the competition if you are under 21.

DID YOU KNOW?
*STEM (science, technology, engineering and maths) and STEAM (science, technology, engineering, arts and maths) are ways of integrating different subjects. A designer, for example, would probably use all these subjects together in a real-world project.

to space exploration and wearable gadgets. Highlights included the 'rock music milkshake machine' which made milkshakes using sound waves from an amplified guitar, and a nanotechnology exhibition called 'Dotography,' consisting of photographs so small – a single pixel! – that they aren't visible without a special microscope attached to your phone.

Every year 500 young finalists of The Big Bang Competition are selected from around the UK to show their ideas at the fair. Ten of them are chosen to pitch their projects to a panel of judges, who award the top science and engineering prizes to their favourite projects. Emily and Josh have joined an impressive list of past winners, including young engineers David Bernstein and Sankha Kahagala-Gamage whose 'Medivest' jacket was designed to predict epileptic episodes using smart materials, and Stuart Chau, Ethan Dunbar Baker and Rogan McGilp whose 'Hot Rod' car was built for Rogan's 13-year-old brother David, who has a disability.

Organizer Mark Titterington believes that the future looks bright because the scientists, engineers and inventors of the future are already producing such exciting work. Hopefully more young people will be inspired to enter the competition by their achievements.

Who knows what exciting new projects will win next year's competition – maybe yours! If you're under 18 and love STEM, check out The Big Bang website to find out how to take part.

6 Answer the questions.
1. Why is Josh's 3D printer described as a 'flat-pack' machine?
2. What was Emily's winning project about?
3. What examples are given of things you can learn about on the stands?
4. Who do the finalists have to pitch their projects to?
5. What is the 'Medivest' jacket?
6. What is the 'Hot Rod' car?

7 Word builder Read the information and answer the questions.

> **NEGATIVE PREFIXES**
> We use negative prefixes such as *in-*, *un-*, *il-* / *ir-* / *im-* and *dis-* to make negative adjectives or nouns.
> expensive ▶ **in**expensive
> ability ▶ **dis**ability

1. How would you make the negative form of these adjectives from the text?

   effective   visible

2. Write the negative form of these words. Use a dictionary to help you.

   advantage   likely   logical
   patient   rational

8 Work in pairs to ask and answer the questions.
1. What STEM / STEAM subjects do *you* study at school?
2. Have you ever designed, invented or discovered something?
3. Do you think you will have a job related to STEM / STEAM in the future?

CRITICAL THINKING
IMAGINE
Look at the article and find examples of winning designs or inventions. Write a list. Imagine you are going to enter a STEM / STEAM competition. Choose one of these categories and imagine a new design or invention.
- Science
- Engineering
- Art and Design

WEB QUEST
Work in groups of three. Find out about the winners of last year's science fairs for young people.

1. **Think** Each choose one of these science fairs:
   - Intel International Science and Engineering Fair
   - European Union Contest for Young Scientists
   - The Big Bang STEM fair in the UK
2. **Investigate** Search online for information about last year's winners. Find out:
   - their name, age and nationality
   - what they invented / designed
3. **Communicate** Share your research with your group. Then present a summary to the class.

TIP! Remember to bookmark the websites you've used, so that it's easy to find them again.

Grammar
The passive

VIDEO: FLIPPED CLASSROOM
Watch the grammar presentation and do the task.

1 Look at the table. Copy and complete the sentences with these words.

- are • aren't • wasn't • were
- will be • won't be

present simple passive

+ The competition **is held** every year.
− Projects from non-students (1) … **accepted**.
? How (2) … the finalists **selected**?

past simple passive

+ The top prizes (3) … **given** to Josh Mitchell and Emily Xu.
− Unfortunately my project (4) … **selected**!
? Where **was** last year's fair **held**?

future passive

+ Next year's finalists (5) … **selected** soon.
− Next year's winners (6) … **announced** until March.
? Where **will** next year's fair **be held**?

2 Copy and complete the present simple passive sentences so they are true for you. Use the affirmative or negative.

At my school …
1 science … (teach) three times a week.
2 students … (encourage) to be innovative.
3 prizes … (award) at the end of the year.
4 the computer room … (use) every day.
5 students … (give) laptops or tablets.

> **ANALYSE**
> We use the passive when the person who does the action isn't mentioned, or isn't important. Translate the sentences in exercise 2. Do you use the passive in your language?

3 Write past simple passive sentences using the information in brackets. Write one negative and one affirmative sentence.

3D printers / invent (last year / 1980s)
3D printers weren't invented last year.
They were invented in the 1980s.

1 The first cars / invent (in England / Germany)
2 iPads / design (by Amazon / Apple)
3 WhatsApp / introduce (in 2018 / 2009)
4 The World Wide Web / create (by an American scientist / a British scientist)

4 Copy and complete the text with the correct form of the verbs in brackets. Use the passive.

CARS: A HISTORY OF INNOVATION

The first car (1) … (design) by the German inventor Carl Benz in 1886. Secretly, it (2) … (test) on a 200 km journey by his wife Bertha, who suggested many improvements! Cheaper cars (3) … (not produce) until 1908, when Henry Ford's first car factories (4) … (open) in the USA. Since then, there have been many different types of cars. Although traditional fuels like petrol and diesel (5) … (still / use) in most of them, greener fuels (6) … (probably / use) more and more in future. Driverless cars are the latest innovation, though in most countries they (7) … (not use) on public roads at the moment. What kind of vehicles (8) … (invent) in the future, I wonder?

5 Order the words to make passive questions. Then choose a gadget that you own, and write true answers to the questions.

was / made / it / When ?
When was it made?
It was made about two years ago.

1 it / What / is / used / for ?
2 designed / it / by / Who / was ?
3 was / made / it / Where ?
4 Where / bought / was / it ?
5 the design / How / be / improved / will / in the future ?

6 Work in pairs. Ask your partner about his / her chosen gadget. Use the questions in exercise 5.

Vocabulary and Listening
Adverb review

LEARNING OUTCOME
✔ Understand technical instructions

DIGITAL VOCABULARY FLASHCARDS

Do the matching exercise to discover the new vocabulary.

absolutely   always   comfortably   easily   extremely
fast   often   quickly   quite   rarely   safely
usually   very   well

1 Read the text. Are you a digital native? Listen and repeat the words in blue. ♪ 38

AM I A DIGITAL NATIVE?

You can be absolutely sure that you are a digital native when you can discover comfortably and easily how new technology works. You always want the latest software and you are usually one of the first to install updates on your phone. You are rarely tricked by internet hoaxes and you delete suspicious emails so you can navigate quickly and safely. You are quite fast at texting and you often use social media to organize your life. On the downside, you get extremely annoyed when devices don't work very well!

2 Copy and complete the table with the adverbs in exercise 1.

adverbs of manner	adverbs of degree	adverbs of frequency

3 **Word builder** Read the information. Find adverbs in exercise 1 that match rules 1–5. Then write an example sentence for each rule.

ADVERBS OF MANNER
1 Most adverbs of manner are formed by adding -ly to the adjective.
2 Adjectives that end in -y change the -y to -i.
3 Some adjectives that end in -e drop the -e in the adverb.
4 Some adverbs have the same form as the adjectives.
5 Some adverbs are irregular.

4 Read rules a–d about adverbs of manner, degree and frequency. Then correct sentences 1–4.

a) The adverbs *hard*, *fast* and *late* all have the same form as the adjective.
b) We don't use adverbs of manner after *look*, *seem* or *feel*.
c) We don't use *very* with extreme adjectives.
d) Adverbs of frequency go after *be*, but before other verbs.

1 Inventors worked hardly to develop computers. ✗
2 Your new tablet looks well! ✗
3 The first computer was very enormous. ✗
4 Nowadays, computers often are tiny. ✗

5 Look at the information and the picture. What do you think the TV show will be about?

TV Review:
Technology Matters!
(Channel 6, 8pm)
In tonight's show we'll learn all about 3D printing, and watch a demonstration.

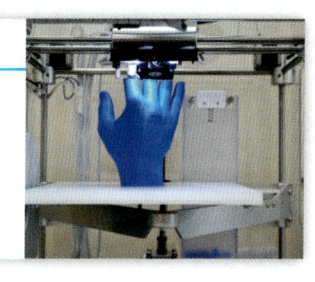

6 Listen to part of the TV show. Write the instructions in the correct order. ♪ 39

1– c *The power cable should be connected.*
a) Click on 'Print'.
b) The plastic should be put on the spool.
c) The power cable should be connected.
d) The printing platform must be levelled.
e) The nozzle height should be selected.
f) The printer should be turned on.

7 Listen again and choose the correct answers.

1 During the programme, they make …
   a) a children's toy.   b) a smartphone case.
   c) a wearable gadget.
2 The material used for the demonstration is …
   a) aluminium.   b) paper.   c) plastic.
3 This 3D printer costs …
   a) £300.   b) £399.   c) £1,369.

Vocabulary basics   Advance your vocabulary ▶ Workbook p107

Social awareness
Virtual classrooms

1 Look at the headline and photo. Which topics do you think you will read about? Then read, listen and check. 🔊 40

- virtual reality
- vocational education
- wearable gadgets
- health and safety
- gaming
- robot teachers

FACT! In 2018, virtual newsreaders were presented by a Chinese news agency. These were created using artificial intelligence (AI) and were built using the voice and facial expressions of real presenters.

| Home | Technology | Business | Health | Entertainment | Family | About us |

Towards a 'virtual' classroom?

New educational technology is developing constantly, and VR (virtual reality) is already a reality in some classrooms.

In China, so far VR software has been installed in some institutions for vocational courses such as tourism and vehicle mechanics. Soon, new VR software will be developed for teaching English, too.

Some of the students had never heard of virtual reality before using the technology in their classes, but they really enjoyed it. One teacher said that students were picking up the new technology very quickly. When schools are in a rural location, VR technology enables students to learn up-to-date skills without needing to study in the city.

Of course virtual reality has been widely used by gamers for years, but it was rarely used in schools because the special headsets were still quite expensive. Now, with cheaper headsets made from cardboard (which are sold for about $10), VR technology is expected to reach a much wider audience over the next decade. Imagine taking a virtual tour down the Nile from the comfort of your geography classroom, or travelling through space before lunch in your science class!

However, despite the potential for fun-filled interactive learning, virtual reality also comes with health warnings. Users are advised to take regular breaks to avoid eye strain, headaches and hearing damage, and the technology isn't recommended for under-13s. In addition, VR is no substitute for interpersonal communication, so it will probably never replace your real teachers!

2 Words in context Find these words in the text. Are they nouns, verbs or adjectives? Match them with definitions 1–5.

> pick up   up-to-date   headset
> eye strain   replace

1 to substitute for a new person or thing
2 to learn a new skill (phrasal verb)
3 VR equipment that you wear over your eyes
4 modern and using the latest ideas
5 a pain in your eyes, for example after reading a lot

3 Copy and complete the sentences with information from the text.

1 In China, some schools have installed …
2 Gamers have used …
3 VR was rarely used in schools because …
4 … probably won't be replaced by VR!

4 Work in pairs. Ask and answer the questions about your country.

1 What kinds of technology are used in your school at the moment?
2 Have you ever used Virtual Reality (VR)? If so, what for? If not, would you like to?
3 In your opinion, what new technology will be used in schools in the future?

VIDEO: CULTURE BYTE
▶ WATCH   Watch the video supplied by BBC.

Grammar
Active and passive voice

1 Look at the table. Do we use *by* in the active or passive voice?

active voice
In the **active** voice, the subject of a sentence is active: it does something.

Chinese students use Virtual Reality.

Virtual Reality is used by Chinese students.

passive voice
In the **passive** voice, the subject is passive: something is done to it.

2 Transform the sentences from active to passive. Only include *by* if necessary.

They sell thousands of VR headsets every year.
Thousands of VR headsets are sold every year.

1 Gamers use virtual reality.
2 More than a billion people speak Chinese.
3 They don't teach Mandarin at my school.
4 People will probably study Chinese more in the future.
5 A lot of businesspeople use Chinese.

3 Choose the correct words. Then listen and check. 🔊 41

FACTS ABOUT VR

» When we think of virtual reality, we often think of gaming, but in fact VR (1) **uses / is used** in many situations that aren't related to gaming, such as medicine, tourism and space travel.
» VR (2) **didn't invent / wasn't invented** by one person – many people (3) **contributed / were contributed** to its development. But the term 'virtual reality' (4) **conceived / was conceived** in the 1980s by the American computer scientist, artist and composer Jaron Lanier.
» The first cardboard headsets (5) **designed / were designed** by engineers David Coz and Damien Henry during Google's 'innovation time' – a programme that (6) **is encouraged / encourages** engineers to spend 20% of their working time on projects of their choice.
» Now that VR headsets can (7) **buy / be bought** very cheaply, they will probably become more and more popular. Who knows how VR will (8) **use / be used** in the future?

CLIL Grammar in context: Literature

4 Complete the quiz with the correct active or passive form of the verbs in brackets.

China
by Jennifer Gascoigne

Quiz: How much do you know about China?
1 What percentage of the world population … (be) Chinese?
   a) 4%   b) 20%
2 Several languages … (speak) in China. Which is the most common?
   a) Cantonese   b) Mandarin
3 For centuries, China was ruled by emperors. Who … (lead) the country now?
   a) the Communist Party   b) an emperor
4 China's tallest building … (build) in the country's largest city. Where is it?
   a) Beijing   b) Shanghai
5 In which year … (the Olympic Games / take place) in Beijing?
   a) 2008   b) 2018
6 The Chinese … (invent) paper, printing and gunpowder. What else was a Chinese invention?
   a) the computer   b) the compass
7 Liu Yang was the first female Chinese astronaut. When … (she / send) into space?
   a) 2012   b) 2017
8 China is in the process of building a space station in orbit. When … (it / complete)?
   a) 2022   b) 2050

5 Answer the quiz questions in exercise 4. Then listen and check your answers. 🔊 42

LITERATURE TASK
Some important innovations related to the history of books were developed in China. Find out about one of these:
• the invention of paper
• woodblock printing
• moveable type printing

Grammar basics | Grammar reference ▶ Workbook p92 | 55

Great innovations

LEARNING OUTCOME
✓ Give a presentation

> Today we're going to give presentations about different inventions. I'm going to talk about mobile phones. Did you know that the first mobiles weighed nearly 1 kg?

TASK Prepare a presentation

1 Read timelines about new technology

2 Understand a factual presentation

3 Write a presentation

4 Give a presentation

NEW TECHNOLOGY

THE INTERNET

1969
four American universities were connected by the ARPA network

1971
the first email was sent by American programmer Ray Tomlinson

1982
the word 'internet' was used for the first time

1989
the World Wide Web was invented by British scientist Tim Berners-Lee

1998
the search engine Google was founded

1999
the internet became available on mobile phones in Japan

2005
the video-sharing website YouTube was founded

2020
it's estimated that the internet will be used by more than 4 billion people worldwide

MOBILE PHONES

1973
the first mobile phone call was made by Motorola in New York

1 ...
the first mobile phone call in Britain was made by Vodafone on 1st January

2 ...
Nokia's 'Cityman' mobile phone was produced

3 ...
SMS text messaging was introduced in Finland

4 ...
the first mobile ringtone was downloaded

5 ...
the first camera phones were sold in Japan

6 ...
the first iPhone was produced by Apple

2025
it's estimated that there will be more mobile phones than people on the planet

1 Read

1 Read the timelines about the internet and mobile phones. What do pictures a–f refer to? Match them with information from the text.

   a) = the first email was sent in 1971

2 Read the internet timeline again. Copy and complete the sentences in your own words.

   1 The ARPA network ...
   2 In 1982, ...
   3 Tim Berners-Lee ...
   4 Google was ...
   5 Mobile phone internet ...
   6 By 2020, ...

2 Listen

3 Read, watch or listen to the extract from Jack's presentation on page 57. Where was the first mobile phone call made? 🔊 43

4 Watch or listen again. Practise your intonation.

5 Listen to the complete presentation. Complete dates 1–6 in the timeline about mobile phones. 🔊 44

> Hello! Today I'm going to talk about the invention and development of mobile phones. Look at my mobile – it's really light, and can probably do everything that can be done on a computer! But early mobile technology was very different, so let's start at the beginning.
> Mobile technology was first developed in the early 1970s, so I'm going to talk about the 70s, 80s and 90s, and then the innovations since the year 2000. I'd be happy to answer any questions at the end of the presentation.
> OK, so our story begins in 1973, when the first mobile call was made by Motorola in New York. But it wasn't until January 1985 that the first mobile call was made in Britain, by Vodafone. After that mobile technology really started to develop.

Communication kit

- In the early / mid- / late (1970s), …
- Then / Next / After that, …
- The following year, …
- It wasn't until (1985) that …
- By (the mid-1990s), …
- Later / (A few) years later, …

6 Listen again and choose the correct answers.

1. The 'Cityman' mobile cost about …
   a) €400   b) €1,000   c) €4,000
2. 'SMS' means '… message service'.
   a) short   b) standard   c) Scandinavian
3. By 2006, … % of mobiles had cameras.
   a) 10%   b) 50%   c) 90%
4. About … iPhones were sold in the first year.
   a) 400,000   b) 1.4 million   c) 4.1 million

7 Look at the Communication kit. Which expressions does Jack use? Watch or listen again to check your answers.

3 Write

8 Prepare a presentation about the history of the internet. Add this information to the timeline on page 56. Then add your own ideas.

1994   the White House website was launched
1997   the term weblog (*blog*) was introduced
2003   iTunes was launched

9 Choose the key information that you want to include in your presentation. Write notes.

4 Communicate

10 Work in pairs. Practise your presentation. Use a stopwatch to time your partner's presentation. Is it too long or too short?

11 Try to improve your presentation. If possible, record it or present it to the class.

COMMUNICATION TIP
GIVING A PRESENTATION

Don't read directly from your notes. Make your presentation interesting by using your own words and varying your tone of voice. Pause from time to time, and don't speak too quickly!

Writing
A formal letter

LEARNING OUTCOME
✔ Write a formal letter of complaint

1 Read Tom's letter and answer the questions.

1 What is the product and where was it bought?
2 What is the problem and how will it be resolved?

A

45 Grove Street
Sheffield
S6 7LP

25th April

B

C The Manager
Mobiles-To-Go
123 Long Street
London NW 8ED

D Dear Sir / Madam,

On 2nd April, I ordered a mobile phone (a Flex400s at £149.99) on your website. My order was placed at 5.40pm, and I received a confirmation email. The money was taken from my account the following day.

Unfortunately, the phone has not arrived. When I called your Customer Help Line, I was told that the phone was sent on 4th April. That is now three weeks ago, and I still haven't received it.

To resolve the situation, I would appreciate it if you could send a new phone or refund my money as quickly as possible. I look forward to your reply and a solution to this problem.

E Yours faithfully,

Tom Sherwood

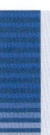

F Tom Sherwood

LOOK!
We often use passive forms when we write in a formal style.

2 **Focus on language** Read the information. Match 1–6 with A–F in the letter.

> **Writing a formal letter**
> When you don't know the person's name:
> 1 start with *Dear Sir / Madam*
> 2 finish with *Yours faithfully*
> Include both your address and their address:
> 3 put your address top right
> 4 put their address on the left
> Don't forget:
> 5 to sign and print your name
> 6 to date the letter

3 Read the letter again and find phrases 1–4. Then copy and complete the sentences with Tom's words.

1 On 2nd April …
2 Unfortunately, …
3 To resolve the situation, …
4 I look forward to …

4 **Focus on content** Read the letter again. Which paragraph …

a) suggests possible solutions?
b) describes the product and when it was bought?
c) explains the problem?

5 Imagine you've bought one of these products and it doesn't work. Write a letter of complaint.

• a tablet   • a laptop   • a games console

Writing kit

1 Plan your letter. Answer the questions in exercise 1 about your product.

2 Write three paragraphs:
 1 describe the product that you bought
 2 explain the problem
 3 suggest possible solutions

3 Useful phrases

I ordered / bought …
Unfortunately, …
To resolve the situation, …
I look forward to your reply.

4 Check your writing.

✔ layout for a formal letter
✔ formal greetings and phrases
✔ check that you've used the correct passive forms
✔ three paragraphs

Study guide ▶ p103   Writing hub ▶ Workbook p120

YOUR IDENTITY

UNIT 6

LEARNING OUTCOMES IN THIS UNIT
- Identify text purpose
- Listen for specific information in a radio discussion
- Have a pairwork debate
- Write a profile of someone you admire

VIDEO: GETTING STARTED
Watch the teenagers talking about identity theft and answer the question.

Vocabulary
Identity theft

1. Read the quiz and check the meaning of the words in blue. Which ones are related to identity theft? Listen and repeat. 🔊 45

2. Do the quiz and check your answers. Do you agree with your result?

HOW SAVVY ARE YOU?

1 How can you avoid being the victim of a scam when buying concert tickets?
a) You can't.
b) You only buy tickets from links on the official website.
c) You pay by credit card, not debit card.

2 Which of these websites makes it more difficult for a fraudster to steal your information?
a) ones that begin https://
b) ones that begin http://
c) both of the above

3 If a wi-fi hotspot requires a password, then it is safe to …
a) log on to your bank account.
b) apply for a loan or check your credit rating.
c) neither of the above.

4 Imagine your uncle goes on a €1,000 spending spree. The interest rate on his credit card is 20%. How much debt must he repay after one year?
a) €1,000   b) €1,020   c) €1,200

5 To avoid identity theft, you should …
a) shred documents that contain personal information.
b) avoid opening junk mail.
c) both of the above.

6 Which of the following are examples of phishing attacks?
a) creating a fake website to trick users into giving personal information
b) sending someone a message on a social networking site with a malicious link
c) both of the above

YOUR SCORE
If you get:

5+ You are very savvy.

3–4 You need to be more aware of finance scams.

0–2 Your digital identity is in danger – take action now!

3. Look at the words in blue in exercise 1 again and answer the questions.
   1. Which ones are verbs?
   2. Which two can be a noun or a verb?
   3. Which ones are compound nouns?
   4. What do you think is the origin of the word 'phishing'?

4. Copy and complete the questions with the correct words. In pairs, ask and answer.
   1. Have you got a … account?
   2. Do you use a social … site? Which one(s)?
   3. Where are the wi-fi … in your town? Do you ever use them?
   4. Do you know anyone who has been the victim of a scam or identity …?

Vocabulary basics

59

Reading
An article and advice

LEARNING OUTCOME
✔ Identify text purpose

1 Read and listen to the text. Who are these people and why does the writer mention them? 🔊 46
- Abby Brown
- Debra
- Mike Haley

2 Read the information. What is the purpose of this text: a, b or c?

> **IDENTIFY TEXT PURPOSE**
> The purpose of the text is the author's reason for writing. The three main purposes are to inform, entertain or persuade.

a) to persuade people to buy a product
b) to entertain or amuse readers
c) to inform readers about the dangers of identity theft

3 Read the text again and choose the correct answers.

1 Abby Brown …
   a) lost her mobile.
   b) left her mobile unattended.
   c) stole a mobile.
2 In 2016, more than 325,000 frauds …
   a) were committed online.
   b) affected teenagers.
   c) were reported.
3 Social networking sites …
   a) can provide personal details for fraudsters.
   b) are safer than email.
   c) are often hacked.
4 You mustn't …
   a) shred personal documents.
   b) prevent identity theft.
   c) choose passwords that are easy to guess.

4 Are the sentences true or false? Find evidence in the text to support your answers.

1 Thieves stole Abby's phone in a restaurant.
2 Abby's mum told their story to a newspaper.
3 A large number of identity crimes in the UK affect young people.
4 Fraudsters sometimes acquire huge debts.
5 You should always open phishing emails.

Stolen phone,

Abby Brown was angry when thieves stole her mobile, but she was devastated the moment she discovered that they had stolen her identity, too. The fraudsters changed Abby's passwords so she couldn't get online, while pretending to be her and sending inappropriate messages to her friends. Abby had left her bag at the beach when she and her friends visited South Harbour in Northumberland.

Fortunately, Abby's mum Debra was able to inform her daughter's friends that Abby's mobile had been hacked. 'Once someone gets their hands on your phone, they get your whole life and you can't stop it,' she told the *Daily Mirror* newspaper. 'My daughter is afraid to go out now because she's scared she will run into these people. They know so much about her!'

Unfortunately, identity theft is getting more and more common. According to the fraud prevention organization Cifas, more than 325,000 frauds were recorded in the UK in 2016, with many of these affecting under-21-year-olds. In the USA, young people are even more at risk due to the fact that they are given social security numbers at birth. If a criminal stole a child's identity, they probably wouldn't realize there was a problem until they tried to open a bank account or apply for a credit card at the age of 18.

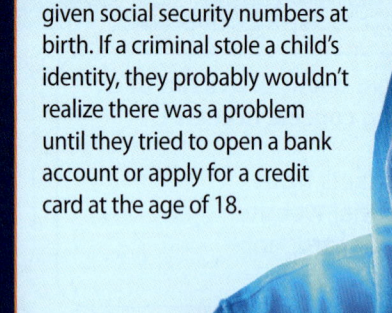

5 **Words in context** Find these words in the text. Are they nouns, verbs or adjectives? Match them with definitions a–e.

> pretend   inappropriate   lock   asset   throw away

a) get rid of something that you don't want
b) property or money that a person owns
c) to close something with a key so that other people can't open it
d) wrong, unacceptable
e) to behave in a particular way because you want someone to believe that something is true when it is not

The longer read ❯ Resource centre

stolen life ...

How do fraudsters get access to your identity? They don't have to steal your phone or hack your computer – they often just exploit personal information from social networking sites. Some also obtain sensitive information through phishing scams (fraudulent emails that appear to be from official organizations). Once they've got the information they need, nothing will stop the criminals from taking out loans in your name, or going on a spending spree and acquiring massive debts.

'We all remember to protect our possessions by locking our house,' Mike Haley of Cifas told the BBC. 'But we don't take the same care to protect our most important asset – our identity.'

What can you do to prevent identity theft?

- You shouldn't share personal information online.
- If you get suspicious junk mail, you mustn't open it – it might be a phishing scam.
- Don't allow others to know your passwords and PIN.
- When you have to choose a new password, don't use something obvious, like your date of birth.
- You should shred all sensitive documents – don't throw them away.

6 Word builder Read the information and answer the questions.

USES OF *GET*
The verb *get* has many different meanings, such as *obtain, become, receive, buy, arrive* or *bring*.
> Identity theft **is getting** more common.
> How do fraudsters **get** access to your information?
> If you **get** suspicious junk mail, don't open it.

1 Find the examples in the text. Does *get* mean *obtain, become* or *receive*?
2 We often use *get* in expressions. What do the expressions 'get online' and 'get your hands on something' mean?

DID YOU KNOW?
Americans are more likely to be victims of identity theft than anyone else – over 791 million identities were stolen in the US in 2016. France was in second place with 85 million identities stolen.

7 Answer the questions.
1 How did the thieves contact Abby's friends?
2 Why do you think Abby's mum spoke to a reporter?
3 How do criminals sometimes steal identities in the USA?
4 How do you think thieves could exploit information from social media sites?
5 What are strong and weak passwords?

8 Work in pairs to ask and answer the questions.
1 Have you or people in your family ever been the victim of ...
   - phone theft?
   - identity theft?
   - social media hacking?
2 What measures do you take to protect your identity and online identity?
3 Do you follow all the steps in 'What can you do to prevent identity theft?'

CRITICAL THINKING

JUDGE
Look at the text again. Find examples of crimes and antisocial behaviour. In your opinion, which ones are the worst? Compare and judge these activities. In your opinion, what should the punishments be?
- phone theft
- identity theft
- uploading photos without permission
- hacking of social media accounts

WEB QUEST
Find out more about how you and your family can protect your personal identities.
1 **Investigate** Search online for 'protect your identity' or 'prevent identity theft'. Take notes about the information and tips you find.
2 **Create** In your own words, make a list of ten top tips to protect your identity.
3 **Communicate** Share your tips with the class.

TIP! You mustn't copy text directly from the internet. Make notes, then rewrite the information in your own words.

Grammar
Modals of ability and possibility, obligation and prohibition

VIDEO: FLIPPED CLASSROOM
Watch the grammar presentation and do the task.

1 Look at the table. Then use the words in blue to complete rules a–f.

present	past
ability and possibility	
+ Criminals **can** steal your identity.	I **could** start using social media when I was 13.
− You **can't** get a credit card until you're 18.	She **couldn't** get online.
obligation and prohibition	
+ You **must** / **have to** shred all personal documents.	Abby **had to** get a new phone.
− You **mustn't** open suspicious emails.	
no obligation	
− The fraudsters **don't have to** hack your computer.	They **didn't have to** go to prison.

a) We use ... and ... to talk about ability or possibility in the present.
b) We use ... and ... to talk about ability or possibility in the past.
c) We use ... or ... for obligation in the present.
d) We use ... for obligation in the past.
e) We use ... for prohibition.
f) We use ... when there is no obligation in the present and ... when there is no obligation in the past.

LOOK!
We don't use **must** / **mustn't** in the past.

2 Copy and complete the sentences with these words. Then match them with rules a–f in exercise 1.

- can • couldn't • don't have to
- had to • has to • mustn't

1 My sister ... wear braces on her teeth now.
2 The dentist says that she ... take them off until she is 16.
3 Fortunately, I ... wear braces.
4 When I was young, I ... go to piano lessons.
5 I ... play the piano very well when I was little.
6 Now I ... play songs by Ariana Grande!

3 Read the text and choose the correct words.

CHANGING APPEARANCE

I think I look quite different now from when I was little. When I was a child I (1) **have to** / **had to** / **must** wear glasses because I (2) **can** / **could** / **couldn't** see very well. Now I (3) **mustn't** / **don't have to** / **didn't have to** wear glasses because I've got contact lenses. Now, I (4) **have to** / **had to** / **can't** wear a school uniform. When I was younger, I (5) **can't** / **don't have to** / **didn't have to** wear a school uniform. I (6) **could** / **must** / **can't** wear my own clothes. But my mum used to choose them for me!

4 Copy and complete the sentences so they are true for you.

When I was five,
1 I had to ...
2 I didn't have to ...
3 I could ...
4 I couldn't ...

Now,
5 I have to ...
6 I don't have to ...
7 I can ...
8 I can't ...

5 Work in pairs. Ask and answer questions about your ideas in exercise 4.

What did you have to do when you were five?
I had to go to swimming lessons. What about you?

Grammar basics | Grammar reference ▸ Workbook p94 | Pronunciation ▸ p125

Vocabulary and Listening
Personal identity

LEARNING OUTCOME
✔ Listen for specific information in a radio discussion

DIGITAL VOCABULARY FLASHCARDS

Do the matching exercise to discover the new vocabulary.

appearance   beliefs   ethnicity   friendship   gender
nationality   peer group   personality   possession
relationship   style   values

1 Look at the diagram and match 1–4 with a–d. Listen and repeat the words in blue. ◁)) 47

1. characteristics that you're born with
2. other people in your life
3. physical things that you can see
4. abstract things about you that you choose

A beliefs, values, personality
B friendships, relationships, peer group
C nationality, ethnicity, gender
D appearance, style, possessions

Who are you?

2 Copy the diagram into your notebook. Add one more idea to each group. In your opinion, which things are most important to your personal identity?

3 **Word builder** Read the information. Does the suffix go at the beginning or the end of a word?

> **NOUN SUFFIXES**
> Many nouns are formed by adding a suffix to the root word (a verb, adjective or other noun), such as *-ity*, *-ness*, *-ment*, *-ship* and *-ance*.
>   happy (adj) – happiness
>   improve (v) – improvement
>   citizen (n) – citizenship

4 Copy and complete the table with the root words.

root word	noun with suffix
relation (n)	relationship
1 … (n)	friendship
2 … (v)	appearance
3 … (adj)	ethnicity
4 … (adj)	nationality
5 … (adj)	personality
6 … (v)	possession

5 Listen to a radio discussion about ID cards. Are Sophie and Miguel for or against? ◁)) 48

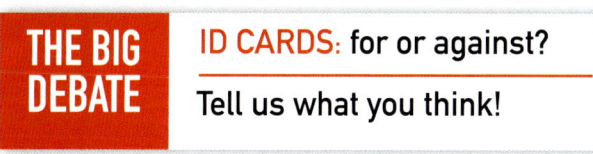

THE BIG DEBATE — ID CARDS: for or against?
Tell us what you think!

6 Read arguments a–f. Which are for ID cards, and which are against? Then listen again. Which arguments do Sophie and Miguel use?

a) Having an ID card makes life easier.
b) It would be very expensive to introduce obligatory ID cards.
c) ID cards help to reduce fraud and fight crime.
d) Your information could fall into the wrong hands.
e) Keeping personal information on a national database goes against civil liberty.
f) You don't have to buy a passport because you can use your ID card to travel in the EU.

7 Listen again and answer the questions.

1. Are ID cards obligatory in the UK?
2. How many countries have obligatory ID cards?
3. What other kind of cards does Sophie mention?
4. When did Miguel get his identity card?
5. Which six pieces of personal information are on Miguel's identity card?
6. Which three examples does Miguel give of bureaucratic procedures where you need to use your ID card?

Vocabulary basics   Advance your vocabulary ▶ Workbook p108   Pronunciation ▶ p125

Life skills
Digital competence

1. What is your digital footprint? Which of these things are part of your digital footprint?
   - websites you visit
   - emails and attachments
   - forum registrations and comments
   - profile posts without privacy settings
   - images and videos you share or download

2. Check the meaning of a–e. Then read the text and match steps 1–5 with headings a–e.
   a) Un-tag yourself
   b) Search yourself online
   c) Delete the cookies
   d) Unsubscribe
   e) Check your privacy settings

3. **Words in context** Find these words in the text. What do they mean?

   > strangers   harmful   reputation
   > rumours   fake news   regret
   > screen-grab

4. Read the text again and answer the questions.
   1. Why is a digital footprint 'like walking through wet concrete'?
   2. What should you do if you find something you don't like when you search yourself online?
   3. What personal qualities should a positive digital footprint reflect?
   4. Are people legally responsible for anonymous online posts?

5. Work in pairs. Choose activity a or b.
   a) Search for each other online. Share your findings and make suggestions for improving your digital presence.
   b) Make real digital 'footprints' – draw round your partner's shoe and write the names of all the digital sites that he / she uses.

FACT! 43% of employers said online postings disqualified candidates.

MANAGING YOUR DIGITAL FOOTPRINT

Your digital footprint is like walking through wet concrete! Complete strangers can see where you've been and what you've done – including that funny picture or comment you uploaded – both now and in the future. Even when you delete a post, it's still stored digitally. Everything you do online contributes to your digital footprint, and all your choices could be harmful to your reputation or future opportunities. So take the time to clean up your digital identity and put your best foot forward …

5 STEPS TO CLEANING YOUR DIGITAL FOOTPRINT

1 …
Check what comes up for yourself online, in both text and images. If you find anything you don't like, ask the site administrator to take it down.

2 …
If you've been tagged in inappropriate photos or videos, ask the person to delete it. To protect your friendships, never tag others without permission.

3 …
Restrict access on social networking sites to people you know. 'Unfriend' anyone you don't know.

4 …
Delete any unused accounts or apps, and unsubscribe from any unwanted email subscriptions.

5 …
Disable cookies or set your browser to delete them when you log out.

CREATING A POSITIVE DIGITAL PRESENCE

- Build your own 'digital identity': if you don't, someone else might!
- Be positive and true – your digital footprint should reflect your beliefs, values and personality. Share your talents, blog about useful things, inspire others! Avoid focusing on your appearance, relationship status, etc.
- 'If I'm anonymous I can't be traced.' FALSE! You're still legally responsible for your actions.
- 'If it's on the internet it must be true!' FALSE! Don't spread rumours or fake news.
- Think long-term: don't post today what you might regret tomorrow (or in five years).
- Remember – anyone can take a screen grab of what you post, so 'if you wouldn't say it face to face, don't say it in the social space!'

Grammar
Modals of deduction

1 Look at the table. Then copy and complete rules a) and b) with *can't*, *must*, *might not*, *could* and *might*.

modals of deduction
1 It **must be** true – I saw it on the national news!
2 It **might not be** true – I read it online.
3 It **could** / **might be** true – I'm not sure.
4 That **can't be** true – it's completely impossible!

a) We use …, … or … when we aren't sure about something.
b) We use … or … when we are sure about something.

2 Copy and complete the sentences with *might*, *must* or *can't*.

Louise

Okan

1 Louise … be in a restaurant.
2 She … be at school.
3 She … be with her brother.
4 Okan … be in Turkey.
5 He … be in England.
6 He … be at the British Museum.

3 Write sentences using the ideas in A, B and C. Then translate them into your language. Which ones are certain?

Living in England could be fun.

A

Living in England	Opening junk mail
Being famous	Being an astronaut
Learning Chinese	Tagging people in photos

B

| must be |
| could / might be |
| can't be |
| might not be |

C

| risky   difficult |
| fun   easy   boring |
| a good / bad idea |

CLIL Grammar in context:
Literature

4 Read the text and choose the correct answers. Then listen and check. 🔊 49

The Invisible Man
by H. G. Wells

HIDDEN IDENTITY

This story is about a man called Griffin who arrives in an English village. He's wearing a big coat, and people can't (1) **seen** / **to see** / **see** his face because it's completely hidden. Griffin's identity is a mystery, and the people in the village think that there (2) **must** / **has to** / **can't** be something strange about their new neighbour. Why (3) **can** / **can't** / **must** they see his face? (4) **Had to** / **Might** / **Can't** he really be invisible?

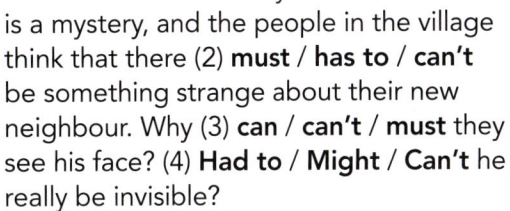

This book is a great mystery story and I enjoyed it very much. I (5) **have to** / **had to** / **must** read it last year in my literature class because we were studying science fiction. I (6) **can** / **must** / **couldn't** believe that the story was originally written in 1897, because some of its themes are quite modern.

Although we (7) **have to** / **mustn't** / **didn't have** to read any other books by H.G. Wells in class, I'm planning to borrow *The War of the Worlds* from the school library as well. I think that (8) **must** / **has to** / **can** be a really exciting story too!

5 Read the text again. Which modals are in the past tense?

LITERATURE TASK
Choose one of these other books by H. G. Wells. Find out what the story is about and write a short synopsis.

The War of the Worlds   *The Time Machine*

UNIT 6

Grammar basics   Grammar reference ▶ Workbook p94   65

Your online identity

LEARNING OUTCOME
✓ Have a pairwork debate

> Today we're going to have a debate about social networking. Does using social media improve our life?

TASK Argue for and against something

1. Read a text about you and your online identity
2. Understand a pairwork debate
3. Prepare your arguments
4. Have a pairwork debate

You and your online identity...

For most of us, social networking has become an integral part of life. According to the Global Digital Report 2018, over three billion people use social media around the world. But does our cyber-identity reflect our real life, or do we create a parallel universe online?

Many of us choose to share only the 'good bits' of our life online, such as pictures of parties and holidays. We can literally 'airbrush' the image of our life – especially with photo-manipulation apps like Instagram. There's even an app which helps people to create a completely fake social life, just to impress others.

All this can lead to 'social media envy', where you think that all your friends must lead really exciting lives. In reality, this is far from the truth. According to a survey by the Future Foundation, 44% of people wish they could be more like the person they describe themselves as on social media.

Perhaps one advantage is that social media can inspire us to enjoy more new experiences in real life – just so that we can share them online!

1 Read

1 Read the text and find words 1–5. Are they nouns, verbs or adjectives? Match them with definitions a–e.

1 share
2 airbrush
3 app
4 fake
5 envy

a) improve an image by hiding defects
b) show or tell other people
c) feeling of discontent when you want what someone else has got
d) software designed to do a particular thing
e) artificial, not genuine

2 Read the text again and answer the questions.

1 How many people use social media?
2 What examples does the author give of the 'good bits' of our online life?
3 How can people 'airbrush' their life?
4 What is 'social media envy'?
5 According to the author, what could be an advantage of social media?

2 Listen

3 Read, watch or listen to the extract from a pairwork debate about social media on page 67. Who is in favour, Oliver or Katy? 🔊 50

4 Watch or listen again. Practise your intonation.

5 Listen to the complete pairwork debate. Which three of these counter-arguments does Oliver use? 🔊 51

1 All your experiences are fake if you only have them to share online.
2 You could have lots of friends on social networking sites, though that doesn't mean you actually see them.
3 Using social media can make people envious and unhappy.
4 You could have no idea about your friends' real lives – they might just share the good bits.

SPEAKING SKETCH

In my opinion, social media motivates you to have more interesting real-life experiences.
Also, I think that you can keep in touch with more friends online than in real life so it makes communication much easier.
Well, with social media, you always know what's going on in your friends' lives.

I'm sorry, but I completely disagree. The way I see it …
I don't see it like that at all. I mean …
That's not how I see it. In my view …

Communication kit
- I'm sorry, but I completely disagree. • I don't see it like that at all. • That's not how I see it.
- I'm afraid I don't agree. • You've made some interesting points, but I see things differently.

6 Look at the Communication kit. Which counter-arguments are used in the Speaking sketch? Listen again to check your answers.

3 Write

7 Prepare for your debate about social media. Copy and complete the table with Katy's arguments in the extract on page 66 and counter-arguments from exercise 5.

Using social media improves our life.

For	Against
Social media motivates you to have more interesting real-life experiences.	All your experiences are fake if you only have them to share them online.

8 Add two more counter-arguments of your own.

4 Communicate

9 In pairs, prepare for your debate. Practise saying your arguments for and against. Use the expressions for giving counter-arguments in the Communication kit.

💬 *In my opinion, …*
💬 *That's not how I see it. …*

10 Have a class debate. Half of you are for and half are against. Which side is more convincing?

! COMMUNICATION TIP
TAKING ROLES IN A DEBATE

Be prepared to take a role which is different from your real opinion. Always write a list of arguments that support your role before the debate, and then try to be convincing!

INTEGRATED SKILLS

Integrated skills ▶ Resource centre

Writing
A personal profile

LEARNING OUTCOME
✔ Write a profile of someone you admire

1 Focus on content Read the profile and match paragraphs 1–4 with a–d.

a) Alper's values and achievements
b) The development of Alper's interests
c) Concluding paragraph
d) Who is Hannah Alper?

Personal details
Born	2003
Nationality	Canadian
Residence	Ontario, Canada
Occupation	Blogger, activist, motivational speaker

Hannah Alper

① **Hannah Alper** is a Canadian blogger, activist and motivational speaker. You might recognize her name <u>because</u> she's already given a TED talk, met inspirational leaders and published a book – all before the age of 15!

② <u>As</u> she launched her blog at the age of nine, Alper is already used to networking. Since then, she has worked with lots of non-profit organizations, such as 'ME to WE' and the World Wide Fund for Nature (WWF). Alper wanted to show that young people could change the world, <u>so</u> she interviewed 19 young role models for her book, *Momentus: Small Acts, Big Change*.

③ Alper's key values include a commitment to young people's rights and social justice and. <u>As a result</u> of this, she has helped to raise awareness and funds for campaigns including anti-bullying, educational equality and environmental issues.

④ <u>Due to</u> her excellent communication skills, Alper has already become a successful public speaker. It can't be easy speaking with confidence in front of so many people! <u>Because of</u> her passionate belief that young people can make a difference, Alper is a role model to many people around the world.

2 Focus on language Read the information. Copy and complete the table with the <u>underlined</u> words from the text.

Connectors of cause and effect

cause	effect
as	so

3 Choose the correct connectors.

Malala Yousafzai is a passionate activist for educational equality. In her homeland, Pakistan, Malala was targeted by extremists (1) **therefore / because / so** she had written a blog about girls' education. (2) **Due to / Because of / As a result**, Malala and her family moved to Britain. When she turned 16, Malala gave a speech about education at the United Nations. The UN declared 12th July 'Malala Day' (3) **as / so / therefore** it is her birthday. Malala wanted to continue campaigning for educational equality (4) **because / so / as a result** she set up the 'Malala Fund' soon after. (5) **Therefore / Due to / So** her campaigning, people around the world are now more aware of these issues.

4 Write a profile of someone you admire.

Writing kit

1 Plan your profile. Answer these questions.
- Who is the person? Is he / she well known?
- How did his / her interests develop?
- What are his / her values and achievements?
- Why do you admire him / her?

2 Write your profile. Use the model and the answers from your plan. Write four paragraphs.
1. introduction
2. development of interests
3. values and achievements
4. conclusion

3 Useful phrases
You might recognize him / her ...
as / because
as a result (of) / due to / because of / so

4 Check your writing.

✔ past and present modals
✔ modals of deduction
✔ connectors of cause and effect
✔ four paragraphs

THAT'S ENTERTAINMENT!

UNIT 7

LEARNING OUTCOMES IN THIS UNIT
- Recognize informal language
- Understand phone calls and messages
- Inform your class about survey results
- Write a report

VIDEO: GETTING STARTED
Watch the teenagers talking about entertainment and answer the question.

Vocabulary
Film-making

1 Read the Careers guide and check the meaning of the words in blue. Which job would you prefer? Listen and repeat. 🔊 52

2 Find words in the Careers guide that mean …
1. all the songs or music played during a film
2. all the people who act in a play or film
3. the written words of a film, play or TV programme
4. a place where a film is made away from a studio
5. a list of all the people that have worked in a film, shown at the beginning or the end

3 Copy and complete the text with these words.
- cast • crew • set • soundtrack • storyboard
- subtitles

Make a film in five easy steps!

① Write a script based on your idea and draw a (a) … for each of the scenes.
② Find the (b) … (director, camera operator, costume designer and make-up artist) and the (c) … (stars and supporting actors).
③ Look for a location, or design the (d) … if you're filming indoors.
④ Shoot your film!
⑤ Afterwards, edit the film. Add sound effects or a (e) … .

(Don't forget to add the credits, and (f) … if it's in a foreign language!)

4 In pairs, ask and answer the questions.
1. Would you like to make a film? Why (not)?
2. What do you think the most difficult parts of making a film would be?
3. Which parts do you think would be the most interesting?

Home | About | Careers | Education | Advice

Careers guide
So you want to work in the movies?

There are plenty of opportunities if you want to be part of a film crew. Here are some of the different roles …

🎥 **Camera operator**
This person records film scenes either in the studio or on location.

👕 **Costume designer**
This job involves designing clothes, shoes and accessories for all members of the cast.

🎬 **Set designer**
This person plans and creates the scenery for a film, play or TV show.

💡 **Lighting technician**
This job involves setting up and operating the lights on a film set or at a concert.

💄 **Make-up artist**
This person works with hair, make-up and special effects to prepare actors for their roles.

🎵 **Words and music**
There are also lots of jobs for writers and musicians. You could write the script or storyboard, plan the sound effects or compose the soundtrack. Specialist translators write the subtitles for foreign films, and the credits are usually written by the producer.

more jobs

Vocabulary basics

69

Reading
A forum

LEARNING OUTCOME

✔ Recognize informal language

1 Read and listen to the text. What does Jack want to find out about? Does he find all the information he's looking for? 🔊 53

2 Read the information. Find at least one example for each of a–d in the text.

> **RECOGNIZE INFORMAL LANGUAGE**
> In informal language we often use:
> a) exclamations
> b) contractions
> c) question tags
> d) agreements with *too / so / neither*

3 Match the sentence beginnings and endings.

1 Jack asked if anyone on the web forum
2 Suki told Jack
3 Jack asked whether
4 Ahmed said that
5 Jack thanked everyone

a) the courses were expensive.
b) could help him.
c) for all the useful information.
d) about the BFI Film Academy courses.
e) his sister was doing a residential course.

4 Words in context Find these words in the text. Match them with definitions a–e.

> buff   hands-on   subsidized
> residential   props

a) objects used in a film or theatre play
b) someone who is very interested in a particular subject
c) involves living at the place where you are studying
d) practical, rather than theoretical
e) paid for in part by the government so that you pay less

5 Answer the questions.

1 Which areas of film-making is Jack particularly interested in?
2 According to Suki, what kinds of hands-on experience can you get on the film course?
3 What did Suki find on the BFI website?
4 What is Ahmed's sister doing on her course?
5 How is Jack going to find out more information?

6 Word builder Read the information and answer the questions.

> **ADJECTIVE + PREPOSITION**
> Some adjectives go with certain prepositions. There aren't any rules, so make a list of them in your notebook.
>
> interested in   well known for   happy with

1 Read the examples. Do you use prepositions with these adjectives in your language?
2 Find these adjectives in the text. Which preposition are they used with?

> involved   committed   excited

7 Work in pairs to ask and answer the questions.

1 Have you ever used an online forum to ask for information or to answer a question?
2 Would you like to do a BFI film course?
3 Do you know about any film courses in your country?

💡 CRITICAL THINKING

DECIDE
Look at the text again. What specific questions does Jack ask? Who answers his questions? Imagine Jack is asking about film courses in your country. Decide on a response.
a) If you know the answer, give information.
b) If you don't know, suggest ways that he could find out more information.

🌐 WEB QUEST

Work in pairs. Find out more about 'netiquette' and write instructions for participating in online forums.

1 **Think** Consider these things and any others that you think are relevant:
- appropriate language
- how to identify yourself   • length of posts
- use of emoticons   • respect for diversity
- how to present your opinions / express your feelings

2 **Investigate** Search for information and take notes. Share your research with your partner.

3 **Create** Prepare instructions for participating in online forums and share with the class.

> **TIP!** Adding 'education' to a web search will often help to return results which are suitable for schoolwork.

70   The longer read ▶ Resource centre

Virtual Teen Forum

Home | Web forum | Register | News | Archive

This conversation: Information about film-making courses

Jack Tuesday 5th May 19.08

Hi all! Can anyone help me? I'm a total film buff and I want to learn more about film-making. A friend told me that she'd heard about some great film courses all around the UK, but she couldn't remember the name of the organization. Has anyone done one of these courses? I'm particularly interested in writing scripts and also set design / visual effects. Thanks for your help!

Suki Tuesday 5th May 19.42

Hi, Jack. I think your friend might mean the BFI – they're well known for their film courses. There are more than 40 courses all over the UK, so there must be one near where you live. I did one and I was really happy with it. They're very hands-on and you can get involved in all areas of film-making, from writing storyboards to doing the lighting or being the camera operator – you really feel like part of a professional film crew. Plus, the teachers are really committed to film and they gave us loads of support and advice. They told us that we were the future of the British film industry!

Jack Tuesday 5th May 19.50

Thanks, Suki. How amazing is that? The courses aren't expensive, are they?

Suki Tuesday 5th May 20.14

No – they're subsidized so you don't have to pay very much. Check out the website for the up-to-date prices. They also have some great video clips by people who've done the course. Everyone was really excited about it and said that you wouldn't regret it! Oh, the only other thing is that you have to be over 16, so you could apply for next year.

Ahmed Tuesday 5th May 20.36

What a great idea! My sister's doing one of the two-week BFI residential courses right now and she loves it there – she told me she was learning loads. She said they'd spent two days filming on location in Oxford, then two days editing in the studio. She's enjoying working with the cast and organizing the costumes and the props. She said they were going on a trip to the BFI cinema in London to watch all the short films they're making. It must be great to see your name in the credits – I think I might go next year!

Jack Tuesday 5th May 20.57

Yes – me too! Thanks, everyone, for all the info. That's really useful! I'm going to have a look at the website now for more information.

DID YOU KNOW?

'*Netiquette*' = *net* + *etiquette*
Netiquette means being polite and respecting other people's views when using online discussion forums.

Grammar
Reported speech

VIDEO: FLIPPED CLASSROOM
Watch the grammar presentation and do the task.

1 Look at the table. Choose the correct words to complete rules a) and b).

direct speech
'I **want** to do a course,' said Jack.

reported speech
Jack said (that) he **wanted** to do a course.

a) **Direct** / **Reported** speech contains the speaker's exact words.
b) In reported speech, the tense is **the same as** / **different from** the direct speech.

2 Look at the table. Then copy and complete the reported speech in sentences 1–7.

tense changes	
direct speech	reported speech
am / is / are →	was / were
present simple →	past simple
present continuous →	past continuous
past simple →	past perfect
present perfect →	past perfect
will or *would* →	would
must or *have to* →	had to
can or *could* →	could

'You must find out about the BFI.'
Suki said that I *had to* find out about the BFI.

1 'You can try all areas of film-making.' She said that I … try all areas of film-making.
2 'I'm interested in visual effects.' Jack said that he … interested in visual effects.
3 'I will look on the website.' He said that he … look on the website.
4 'My sister has done a film course.' Ahmed said that his sister … a film course.
5 'I want to go, too.' He said that he … to go.
6 'I'm hoping to apply with a friend.' He said that he … to apply with a friend.

🔍 ANALYSE
Can you omit *that* when you use reported speech in your language?

3 Rewrite Suki's sentences using reported speech.

'I did a film course.'
Suki said (that) she had done a film course.

1 'I really enjoyed it.'
2 'The teachers are very good.'
3 'I haven't done a residential course yet.'
4 'I'll apply next year.'
5 'I'm going to work in the film industry.'

4 Read the information in the table. Then rewrite Kate's post in reported speech, making any necessary changes.

changes to time expressions
direct speech → reported speech
today → that day
tomorrow → the following day / the day after
next week → the following week / the week after
yesterday → the previous day / the day before
last week → the previous week / the week before
four years ago → four years before

changes to other words
here → there   this → that   these → those

I'm camping at the Blueberry Rock Festival. I arrived two days ago. It's amazing here! I'm going to see my favourite band this evening. They're going to play again tomorrow. I hope it won't rain!

Kate said (that) she was camping at …

5 In pairs, ask and answer the questions. Then report your partner's answers to the class.

Mo said that he'd never been to a music festival.

1 Have you ever been to a music festival?
2 Do you download music?
3 Did you listen to music on your way to school today?
4 Will you work in the music industry?

Vocabulary and Listening
Reporting verbs

LEARNING OUTCOME
✔ Understand phone calls and messages

DIGITAL VOCABULARY FLASHCARDS

Do the matching exercise to discover the new vocabulary.

admit   agree   ask   complain   convince   invite   offer
promise   refuse   say   suggest   tell

1 Read the magazine article. Why was the festival stopped? Listen and repeat the words in blue. ◉ 54

STORM CHAOS
at rock festival

Torrential rain caused chaos at Blueberry Rock Festival, where organizers **admitted** that they weren't prepared for the storms. After some bands **complained** that it wasn't safe to perform, the organizers **asked** everyone to leave the festival early on Sunday morning.

Rock group Red Box **refused** to finish their performance on Saturday night. Lead singer Harry **said** that the organizers had **convinced** them to play, but then lightning struck the electrical equipment. They **told** people not to panic as they abandoned the stage.

Festival organizers **offered** to organize an extra concert in August and they **invited** all the bands to return. They also **promised** to give compensation. They **agreed** to refund half the ticket price, and **suggested** that people should check their website for more information.

2 Word builder Read the information. Then copy and complete the table with the infinitive of the verbs in blue in exercise 1.

> **LEARNING VERB PATTERNS**
> Reporting verbs can follow three patterns: it's important to learn how they are used.
> verb + infinitive with *to*
> verb + object + infinitive with *to*
> verb + *that*

verb + infinitive with *to*	verb + object + infinitive with *to*	verb + *that*
agree to …	invite someone to …	complain that …

3 Rewrite the sentences in reported speech. Make any necessary changes.

1 'Let's go to the extra concert.' (we / agree)
2 'I'll get the tickets!' (I / offer)
3 'Will you bring your sister?' (he / ask)
4 'Get four tickets!' (he / tell)
5 'My cousin is going to come, too.' (he / say)

4 Look at the information. Who can get free tickets? How?

BLUEBERRY ROCK FESTIVAL
Did you have to leave the festival due to the bad weather?

Call our Ticket Line on **0801 776332** to reserve tickets for the **FREE** extra concert on **Saturday 19th August!**

5 Listen to five short phone calls or messages. Match 1–5 with a–e. ◉ 55

a) an informal voicemail message
b) a pre-recorded message
c) a conversation on a landline
d) an informal mobile conversation
e) a call to the Ticket Line

6 Listen again. Are the sentences true or false? Correct the false sentences.

1 Emily and Jack agreed to meet at 7.30.
2 The Ticket Line was very busy.
3 Emily asked if she could reserve two tickets.
4 Jack rang to say that he would be late.
5 Jack's mum told Emily that he hadn't left yet.

7 Choose the correct answers.

1 Emily and her friends are going to the concert by **bus** / **train**.
2 Emily can't get through to the Ticket Line because it's **closed** / **busy.**
3 Emily must **pay by credit card** / **show ID** before collecting the tickets.
4 Jack was late because his mum asked him to return a **DVD** / **library book** on the way.

Vocabulary basics   Advance your vocabulary ▶ Workbook p109

Social awareness
Entertainment and technology

FACT! Around the world, almost 2.4 billion people use a smartphone.

1 Look at the infographic. What is 'entertechment'?

2 Read and listen to the text. What do these numbers refer to? 🔊 56
- 750,000
- 292
- one billion
- 27
- 2,200,000

3 **Words in context** Find these words in the text. What do they mean? Are they nouns, verbs or adjectives?

> inseparable   overwhelming
> viewers   streaming   e-sports

4 Are the sentences true or false? Find evidence in the text to support your answers.
1. Music streaming sites have more than 100 million subscribers.
2. Worldwide, more gamers use consoles than PCs.
3. More than 70% of cinema tickets are bought by over-25s.
4. The average user makes 44 website visits each month.
5. 17% of books sold are e-books.

5 Work in pairs. Ask and answer the questions about your country.
1. How do you and your friends usually watch films, read books and listen to music?
2. Is gaming popular in your country? And e-sports?
3. Which websites and apps do you and your friends use most?

VIDEO: CULTURE BYTE Watch the video supplied by BBC.

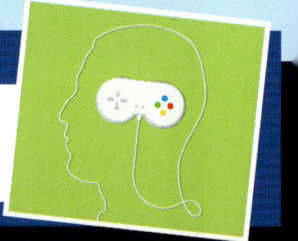

ENTERTAINMENT + TECHNOLOGY = 'ENTERTECHMENT'!

MUSIC
More than 112 million people subscribe to music streaming sites worldwide.

Worldwide, more than 750,000 tracks are streamed on Spotify every minute.

GAMING
There are about 1.8 billion gamers in the world (62% use a PC and 56% a console).

48% of gamers play social games

More than 292 million people worldwide view and play e-sports.

CINEMA, TV AND STREAMING
In 2016, only 29% of cinema tickets were bought by 12–24-year-olds.

Worldwide, Netflix users collectively view more than one billion hours per week.

Out of 194 available channels, the average viewer watches no more than 19 channels.

INTERNET AND APPS
The average user makes 96 website visits per month (but spends 44% of the time on just five websites).

The average user has 27 apps (but spends 79% of the time on just five apps).

300 hours of video are uploaded to YouTube every minute.

BOOKS AND E-BOOKS
Sales of real books up 5% and sales of e-books down 17% last year.

Approximately 2,200,000 new books are published worldwide every year.

If someone asked you how much of your entertainment involved technology, what would you say? Most of us would probably agree that due to smartphones and tablets, technology and entertainment are often inseparable. Nowadays, nearly everyone carries a portable 'entertechment hub', which is full of promises to entertain us constantly. But the huge choice offered by technology can be overwhelming. For example, when asked whether they used all 194 TV channels in one country, viewers admitted that they'd never watched more than 19. In addition, technology has made us all potential entertainers: uploading videos, sharing photos and suggesting playlists.

Grammar
Reported questions

1 Look at reported questions a–d in the table. Then answer the questions.

reported questions
wh- / how questions
'How many channels **do** people **watch**?' a) They asked how many channels people **watched**. 'Which apps **have** you **used**?' b) They asked which apps I **had used**.
yes / no questions
'**Do** you **buy** music?' c) They asked if / whether I **bought** music. 'Have you **played** e-sports?' d) They asked if / whether I **had played** e-sports.

1 Do we use question marks in reported questions?
2 Are the tense changes the same as in reported statements?
3 When do we use *if* / *whether*?

2 Choose the correct words.

Guess what! A famous actor came to our school yesterday, and we asked him …
1 **if he liked** / **does he like** the James Bond films.
2 how many films **had he made** / **he had made**.
3 what **will be his next film** / **his next film would be**.
4 where **he lived** / **did he live**.
5 **would he** / **if he would** give us his autograph.

3 Read the reported questions in exercise 2 again. Then write them in direct speech.

1 *'Do you like the James Bond films?'*

CLIL Grammar in context: Literature

4 Read the text and choose the correct answers. Then listen and check. 🔊 57

Casino Royale
by Ian Fleming

THE FIRST JAMES BOND STORY

At the moment I'm reading *Casino Royale*, which is the first James Bond story. It's full of intrigue, crime and deception. A friend of mine (1) **suggested that I should** / **to** / **me to** read it because I'm a big fan of the James Bond films.

At the start of this story, Secret Agent 007 was sent to France. His boss told him (2) **go** / **to go** / **going** to a casino and play against the Russian agent, Le Chiffre. He explained that Bond (3) **has to** / **must** / **had to** beat Le Chiffre and win all his money. He (4) **told** / **said** / **explained** him that his assistant (5) **will** / **would** / **is going to** be the beautiful spy, Vesper Lynd.

I'm only about half-way through the book so I don't know the end of the story yet. My friend said that I (6) **will be** / **would be** / **am** surprised, but when I asked her (7) **if** / **what** / **whether** happened, she told (8) **me** / **to me** / **me to** wait and see!

LITERATURE TASK
Find out more about the James Bond stories.
• Where was Ian Fleming born?
• Where did he write *Casino Royale*?
• How many James Bond books did he write?
• What other jobs did Ian Fleming do?

An entertainment survey

LEARNING OUTCOME
✓ Inform your class about survey results

> Today we're going to carry out a class survey about entertainment. How often do you go out with your friends?

TASK Do a survey

1 Read an entertainment survey
2 Understand a survey
3 Practise a survey
4 Inform your class about survey results

Entertainment survey

Name: Katy Smith
Age: 15

1 How often do you usually go out with your friends?
a) once or twice a week ○
b) three or four times a week ✓
c) more than four times a week ○
Comments: I usually go out on Fridays and Saturdays, and once or twice in the week.

2 Do you ever go to the cinema?
a) No, there isn't a cinema where I live. ○
b) Yes, once or twice a month. ✓
c) Yes, more than twice a month. ○
Comments: I also watch films at my friends' houses.

3 Have you ever been to the theatre?
a) Yes, to see a play. ✓
b) Yes, to see a concert or performance. ○
c) No, I haven't. ○
Comments: I've seen a few plays and a ballet at the theatre – with my parents!

4 Are you interested in computer games?
a) No, I never play computer games. ○
b) Yes, I play occasionally. ○
c) Yes, I'm a frequent gamer. ✓
Comments: I've got a PlayStation 4.

5 How many hours do you spend in front of a screen?
a) Less than 7 hours per week. ○
b) 7–15 hours per week. ✓
c) More than 15 hours per week. ○
Comments: I also do sports, so I don't spend all my time in front of a screen!

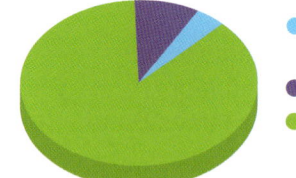

- less than 7 hours per week
- 7–15 hours per week
- more than 15 hours per week

If you have any additional comments, please write them here:
I'd love to go to more concerts, but there isn't a concert venue in my town.

---

1 Read

1 Read the survey. How many hours does Katy spend in front of a screen? Do you spend more or less time than this?

2 Read the survey again. Then copy and complete the sentences.
1 Katy said she went out … a week.
2 She said she went to the cinema … a month.
3 She told Jack that she … at the theatre.
4 She said that she … a PlayStation.
5 She said there wasn't a … in her town.

2 Listen

3 Read, watch or listen to the extract from a survey on page 77. When does Emily go out?))) 58

4 Watch or listen again. Practise your intonation.

5 Listen to the complete survey. Are the sentences true or false? Correct the false sentences.))) 59
1 Jack said the survey would take twenty minutes.
2 Emily said she often watched films online.
3 Emily said she had never been to the theatre.
4 She said she wasn't interested in computer games.
5 Emily said she spent less than ten hours a week in front of a screen.

SPEAKING SKETCH

Hello, Emily! I'm doing some research into entertainment. Could I ask you a few questions?	Sure, no problem.
Great, thanks. It won't take longer than five minutes. I'll be taking some notes – is that OK?	Yes, that's fine.
OK, let's get started! First, could you tell me how old you are, please?	Yes, I'm 15.
OK, and could you tell me how often you go out with your friends?	Oh, probably a couple of times a week – once at the weekend and once during the week.
So you go out about twice a week then – is that correct?	Yes, on average.

Communication kit
- I'm doing some research into …
- Could I ask you a few questions?
- It won't take longer than five minutes.
- I'll be taking notes – is that OK?
- OK, let's get started!
- Could you tell me …
- Would you mind telling me …?

6 Look at the Communication kit. Which phrases are used in the Speaking sketch? Listen again to check your answers.

3 Write

7 Prepare your answers to the questions in the survey. Choose a, b or c and write your own comments in your notebook.

8 Prepare to interview your partner. Change survey questions 1–5 into indirect questions.

1 Could you tell me how often you usually go out with your friends?

4 Communicate

9 Work in pairs. Interview your partner to find out his / her answers to the survey. Write the answers in your notebook.

I'm doing some research into …

10 Tell the class about your interview. Use reported questions and reported speech.

I asked Javier how often he went out with his friends, and he told me that …

11 Compile all the survey results in your class.

15 people said they usually went out twice a week …

! COMMUNICATION TIP
ASKING INDIRECT QUESTIONS

Use indirect questions to make questions or requests more polite. The word order in indirect questions is the same as in reported questions.

INTEGRATED SKILLS

Writing
A report

LEARNING OUTCOME
✓ Write a report

A REPORT ABOUT ENTERTAINMENT FACILITIES IN OUR TOWN

1. This report outlines the results of a survey about entertainment for young people in our town. 30 students aged 15–16 were asked about the facilities they use now, and the new facilities they would like to have.

2. The majority of those questioned said that there weren't enough facilities for young people. Only one in ten people thought the facilities were sufficient. More than half of those interviewed agreed that there should be a new cinema, and a large proportion (40%) said they would like to have a concert venue here, too. 20% said they also wanted new sports facilities, such as a skatepark.

3. To sum up, this survey shows that young people aren't completely satisfied with the entertainment facilities in our town. They would like to have new facilities, such as a multi-screen cinema, a concert venue and a skatepark. I suggest that we should send this report to the town council so that they can take our opinions into account.

1 Focus on content Read the report. Which paragraph …

a) has a summary of the results and provides recommendations?
b) introduces the purpose and content of the report?
c) gives some statistics from the survey?

2 Focus on language Read the information. Which expression refers to the biggest number? Which refers to the smallest number?

> **Expressing statistics**
> the majority   one in ten
> nine out of ten
> more than half
> a large proportion   20%

3 Express each statistic in a different way.

30% = three out of ten

1 55%
2 one in four
3 70%
4 less than half
5 99%
6 three quarters

4 Write a report based on the results of your class survey from page 77.

Writing kit

1 Plan your report.
- Collect all the data from your class survey.
- Analyse the results.

2 Write your report using three paragraphs. Use the model report to help you.
1 introduction
2 results of the survey
3 conclusion and your recommendations

3 Useful phrases

This report outlines …
… of those questioned said / thought / agreed …
To sum up, …
I suggest …

4 Check your writing.

- ✓ phrases for expressing statistics
- ✓ use reporting verbs and the correct tenses in reported speech
- ✓ three paragraphs

Study guide ▶ p105   Writing hub ▶ Workbook p124

PERSUADING PEOPLE

UNIT 8

LEARNING OUTCOMES IN THIS UNIT
- Guess meaning from context in a text
- Understand numbers and prices in radio adverts
- Use persuasion in a presentation
- Write a for and against essay about online advertising

VIDEO: GETTING STARTED
Watch the teenagers talking about advertising and answer the question.

Vocabulary
Advertising

1 Make a list of all the places where you see adverts. How many ads* do you think you see every day?

on the internet, in magazines, …

* ad = advert = advertisement

2 Check the meaning of the words in the box. Use a dictionary to help you. Are they nouns, verbs or adjectives? Listen and repeat. ◉ 60

> ad agency   advert
> advertising campaign   brand
> celebrity   consumer   eye-catching
> go viral   hype   jingle   online ads
> peer pressure   persuasive
> target audience

3 **Word builder** Read the information and answer the questions.

> **COMPOUND NOUNS AND ADJECTIVES**
> We make compound nouns and adjectives when we put two words together. The two words are sometimes written separately and sometimes with a hyphen.
>
> eye-catching (adjective)
> ad agency (noun)

1. Which other expressions in exercise 2 are compound words?
2. Are they compound nouns or compound adjectives?

4 Find words in exercise 2 that mean …
1. a famous person, especially in entertainment
2. someone who buys and uses products or services
3. a short slogan or tune designed to be easily remembered
4. a product or group of products that are made by one particular company
5. the use of intensive publicity or promotion to create interest
6. the influence that other people of your age have on the way you behave or dress
7. attractive or unusual, so you notice it
8. good at making people believe what you want them to

5 Choose the correct words.

CAN YOU REMEMBER …

1. an eye-catching **advert** / **target** from your childhood?
2. a **hype** / **jingle** that you've heard on the radio or on YouTube?
3. a well-known **peer pressure** / **ad agency** in your country?
4. a **consumer** / **celebrity** who advertises a sports brand?
5. an online ad which has gone **viral** / **persuasive** recently?

Taste the summer

6 Work in pairs. Ask and answer the questions in exercise 5.

💬 *Can you remember …?*   💬 *Yes, I can. I remember …*

Vocabulary basics

79

Reading
An article with comments

LEARNING OUTCOME
✔ Guess meaning from context in a text

1 Read and listen to the text. Do you know where these places are? How are they relevant to the article? 🔊 61
- Clapham Common Underground Station
- Virginia • Atlanta, Barcelona and Cape Town
- Times Square

2 Words in context Find these words in the text. Are they nouns or verbs? Match them with definitions a–e from the text.

> bombard   billboard   raise (money)
> supporter   infrastructure

a) the structures and facilities needed for society to operate
b) to give someone so much information that it is difficult to deal with
c) someone who supports a particular idea or cause
d) to collect money for a particular purpose
e) a large board for adverts in an outside public place

3 Read the information. Then guess the meaning of these words and expressions from the text.
- advertising takeover • rescue cat
- marketing stunt • cat-crazy
- copy-cat campaign • captive audience

> **GUESS MEANING FROM CONTEXT**
> It isn't always possible to check a word in the dictionary (for example, in an exam), so it's important to guess its meaning using the context of the sentence and text.
> - Think about the meaning of the words around it, and the type of word it is.
> - Think about what you already know about the subject of the text.

4 Copy and complete the sentences to make definitions for these cat-related words.
1. C.A.T.S. is an acronym which means …
2. A rescue cat is a cat that needs …
3. A cat-crazy person is a person who …
4. A copy-cat campaign is a campaign which …

HOME | BLOG | RECENT | FORUM

PURRFECTLY
FELINE FRIENDS TAKE OVER

Nowadays it seems we can't go anywhere without being bombarded with adverts for things we don't need. That's why a group of friends in London formed 'C.A.T.S.' (the Citizens Advertising Takeover Service), to create a space where people could take a break from all the ads. For two whole weeks, they replaced all 68 billboards at Clapham Common Underground Station with pictures of cats, cats … and more cats! They chose cats because they thought it would help the story to go viral. Plus, most of the cats on the billboards were real rescue cats which needed new homes, so this was a good way to lend a hand.

James Turner, founder of Glimpse, the group that organized the campaign, explained that they weren't trying to make money or sell anything. 'This isn't a clever marketing stunt for a pet food brand,' he told *The Independent* newspaper. 'The people behind it are volunteers who raised the money using Kickstarter.' In total, more than 700 people donated £23,000 to the crowd-funding campaign. Every supporter received a reward – from a cat-themed app for a £5 donation, to a photographic portrait of the pet whose owner gave £2,500. One cat-crazy supporter even flew to London from Virginia, USA, to see his pet on the giant billboard in the station!

WHAT DO YOU THINK? SHOULD ADVERTISING

Anny03 — 22 May @ 16:30
Yes – it's ugly to see ads everywhere. And it isn't fair because we can't choose whether to look at them or not – we're a captive audience!

CityBoy — 22 May @ 16:52
Because of the fact that money from advertising is used to pay for public infrastructure, I think it's something which we have to accept. It benefits consumers as well as companies.

5 Answer the questions.
1. How many billboards at the tube station were replaced with pictures of cats?
2. How long were the cat pictures in the station?
3. Who is James Turner?
4. How much money was raised by the crowd-funding campaign?
5. How much money did supporters have to give to get a photographic portrait of their own pet?

The longer read ▶ Resource centre

DID YOU KNOW?
Studies show that the average American is exposed to between 4,000 and 10,000 brand adverts every day.

PERSUASIVE...
LONDON UNDERGROUND

The people behind C.A.T.S. just want us all to think about the power that ad agencies and brands have over us. They would like us to imagine a world where public spaces make us feel positive. 'We know this is a silly project,' adds James. 'But what if we did this in every major city in the world? Cats everywhere! From all this madness something amazing could happen.' And apparently, 'copy-cat' campaigns are planned in Atlanta, Barcelona and Cape Town!

BE BANNED IN PUBLIC SPACES?

GreenGreg — 22 May @ 17:13
Ads can be so persuasive. They definitely shouldn't target young kids at an age when they're much too susceptible to peer pressure.

CatLover — 22 May @ 18:22
No way! Not only do adverts make you smile, but they also add colour to ugly places. Imagine Times Square without those huge eye-catching signs!

6 Answer the *Why ...?* questions with *because* and ideas from the text.
1 Why did a group of friends form C.A.T.S.?
2 Why did they choose to put photos of cats on the billboards?
3 Why did people donate to the campaign?
4 Why did one supporter fly to London?
5 Why do the people at C.A.T.S. want us to think about advertising?

7 Word builder Read the information and answer the questions.

> **VERB + NOUN COLLOCATIONS**
> Certain verbs and nouns are often used together, for example:
> take a break   lend a hand
> receive a reward

1 Find the examples in the text. Match them with definitions a–c.
a) get a prize or gift
b) have a rest
c) help someone

2 Which other verbs collocate with the nouns above? Choose the correct verbs.
1 **be** / **have** a break
2 **give** / **take** (someone) a hand
3 **have** / **get** a reward

8 In pairs, ask and answer the questions.
1 Are there adverts on public transport where you live?
2 Where do you see ads on an average day in your town?
3 Do you think it was a good idea to have pictures of cats instead of ads? Why (not)?

CRITICAL THINKING

CATEGORIZE
Read the comments. Categorize the arguments *for* and *against* banning ads in public places. Can you think of any more arguments?
Decide whether you are for or against banning ads in public places. Compose your own comment for the Comments section.

WEB QUEST

Works in pairs. Find images and videos about the C.A.T.S. takeover at Clapham Common tube station.

1 **Investigate** Each choose either images or videos. Search online specifically for either images or videos.
2 **Communicate** Share your results with your partner. Select the best images and videos to show to the class.

TIP! Remember to use the options under the search bar to look specifically for 'images' or 'videos'.

Grammar
Relative pronouns

VIDEO: FLIPPED CLASSROOM
Watch the grammar presentation and do the task.

1 Read sentences a–e in the table. Check the meaning of the relative pronouns. Then answer the questions.

who, which, where, when, whose
a) C.A.T.S. was a campaign **which** / **that** replaced adverts with photos of cats.
b) It was set up by a group of friends **who** / **that** lived in London.
c) They wanted to create a space **where** people could take a break from adverts.
d) We're bombarded with adverts **whose** slogans have become part of popular culture.
e) Advertisers shouldn't target children at an age **when** they're susceptible to peer pressure.

1 Do relative pronouns come before or after the noun they describe?
2 Which relative pronoun do we use for possession?
3 Which relative pronoun do we use for …
  people? things? places? time?
4 When can we use *that*?

2 Copy and complete the questions with the correct relative pronouns. Then listen and check. Ask and answer the quiz questions. 🔊 62

QUIZ — What's the name of …
- the country (1) … H&M was set up?
- the South Korean brand (2) … produces Galaxy phones?
- the tech company (3) … logo is a fruit?
- the actor (4) … promotes Nespresso coffee?
- the company (5) … owns YouTube?
- the city (6) … you can see the Piccadilly Circus adverts?

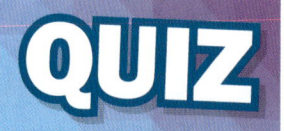

Indefinite pronouns

3 Look at the sentences in the table. Then choose the correct words in rules a–c.

some-, any-, no- compounds
You can't go **anywhere** without seeing adverts.
There's **nowhere** you can go to avoid the ads.
There should be **somewhere** you can go without advertising.
Is there **anywhere** you can go without seeing adverts?

a) We usually use *some-* in **affirmative** / **negative** sentences.
b) We use *any-* in **affirmative** / **negative** sentences and questions.
c) We use *no-* with **affirmative** / **negative** verbs.

4 Match 1–3 with a–c. Which pronouns do we use in questions?

1 people   a) something, nothing, anything
2 places   b) someone, no one, anyone
3 things   c) somewhere, nowhere, anywhere

5 Copy and complete the dialogue with the pronouns in exercise 4.

A: Hi, Ben! Are you doing (1) … on Saturday afternoon?
B: No, I don't think so. (2) … in particular!
A: Do you want to come shopping with me? I need to buy (3) … for Rob's birthday.
B: OK. Let's meet (4) … for a coffee first.
A: Let's meet at the Green Café. (5) … told me their cupcakes are delicious.
B: Sounds great! See you there at three o'clock?

6 Complete the sentences so they are true for you. Talk about your sentences with your partner.

1 … is somewhere I often go shopping.
2 I never buy anything which …
3 I don't know anyone who …
4 … is someone who I really admire.

🔍 ANALYSE

In English, we don't use 'double negatives'.
~~There isn't nothing to do.~~ ✘
There's nothing to do. ✔
What about in your language?

---

82 | Grammar basics | Grammar reference ▸ Workbook p98 | Pronunciation ▸ p125

Vocabulary and Listening
Easily confused verbs

LEARNING OUTCOME
✔ Understand numbers and prices in radio adverts

DIGITAL VOCABULARY FLASHCARDS

Do the matching exercise to discover the new vocabulary.

borrow   earn   hope   lend   remember   remind   see
spend   wait   waste   watch   win

1 Match the verbs with meanings a) and b). Listen and repeat the words in blue. 🔊 63

1. **spend** / **waste**
   a) use money to pay for things
   b) use more of something than is necessary
2. **hope** / **wait**
   a) stay in one place because something is going to happen
   b) want or expect something to happen
3. **win** / **earn**
   a) receive money for work that you do
   b) finish first in a competition
4. **borrow** / **lend**
   a) use something that belongs to someone else, and promise to return it later
   b) give someone something for a short period of time
5. **see** / **watch**
   a) look at something for a period of time
   b) notice something or someone
6. **remember** / **remind**
   a) tell someone again about something that they used to know
   b) bring to mind a fact you knew before

2 Choose the correct verbs. Then write true answers.

1. Have you ever **won** / **earned** a prize?
2. Did you **see** / **watch** anything on TV last night?
3. Do you ever **borrow** / **lend** books from the library?
4. How long would you **hope** / **wait** for friends if they were late?
5. How do you **remember** / **remind** new English words that you learn?
6. How much do you **spend** / **waste** on your mobile phone every month?

3 Work in pairs. Ask and answer the questions in exercise 2.

💬 *Have you ever ...?*
💬 *Yes, I have. I ...*

4 Look at pictures a–f. What kind of product or service are they related to?

5 Listen to adverts 1–5. Match them with five of the pictures in exercise 4. 🔊 64

6 Listen to the adverts again. What do these numbers and prices refer to?

14.99 = pounds (the price of a mega-pizza)

1 20   2 300   3 40
4 30   5 3

7 Answer the questions.

Which advert ...
a) is trying to persuade you to change your behaviour?
b) explains that you can order online or by phone?
c) is promoting something that you can't do / buy yet?
d) is selling a product with a 50% discount?
e) mentions a promotion where you can win something?

Vocabulary basics   Advance your vocabulary ▶ Workbook p110

Life skills
Critical thinking

FACT! Some web browsers allow you to control the ads you see.

1. Think about adverts you remember. What makes them memorable? Write a list.

   slogans, humour, jingles, …

2. Read the text. How many of your words in exercise 1 did you find?

3. **Words in context** Find these words in the text. What do they mean?

   catchy   swipe   mood
   bargain   gender

4. Match questions a–e with the key words in the text.
   - type • tone • focus • attraction
   - objective

   a) Who is the target audience?
   b) Is it an audio / video / interactive ad?
   c) What attracts the consumer's attention?
   d) Is it funny / emotional / serious?
   e) Is the ad for a specific product or a brand?

5. Work in pairs. Choose an advert from a magazine or website. Analyse your ads using the questions in the text. In your opinion, do the ads achieve their objectives?

Analysing adverts

Have you ever seen an ad that suddenly appeared on your screen to remind you about something you were looking at the day before?

Now, adverts are increasingly integrated into our daily lives, and targeted to specific users. Advertisers 'track' our movements every time we interact online – clicking on links, talking to 'chatbots', helping ourselves to 'free' content.

The internet is so full of advertising that we need to put our critical thinking skills into action! Next time you see an ad, ask yourself the following questions …

1 What TYPE of advert is it?
What can you see / hear? Are there any eye-catching images, logos or catchy jingles? Is it interactive – can you click / swipe / play?

2 What's the TONE?
What's the general 'mood' of the ad – is it funny or serious, silly or stylish? Is the language informative, emotional or both? Is there a bigger 'story', such as ambition, adventure or love?

3 What's the FOCUS?
Is the company hoping to earn your trust and persuade you to commit to the brand over time? Or are they just selling this product?

4 What's the ATTRACTION?
Does the ad make you feel that you're getting a bargain (e.g. 'buy one get one free')? Or do you identify yourself with the people in the ad ('cool', 'eco-friendly', etc)? If there are celebrities in the ad, why might that be?

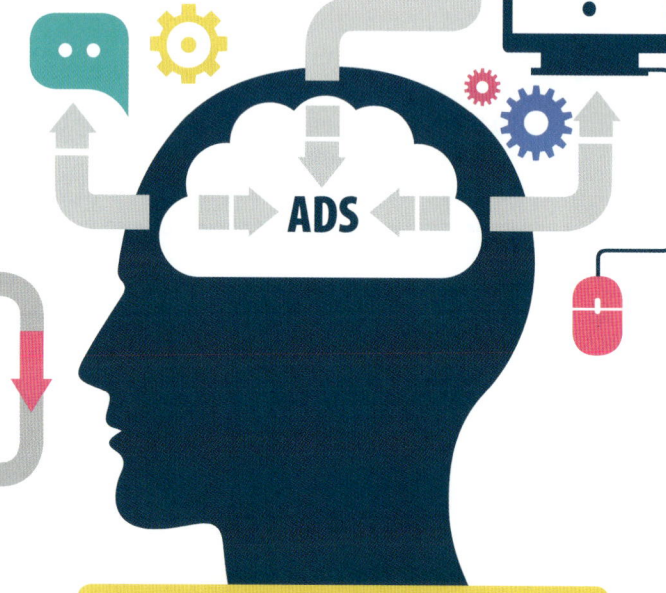

5 What's the OBJECTIVE?
Does the ad target you specifically (for example, by age / gender / location)? If you use this product, will you become a 'walking advert' (e.g. by wearing clothing with a logo or carrying a particular brand of technology)?

Do you think the advert achieves its objectives? Does it make you want to spend money, and will you remember the advert and / or the brand?

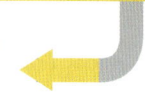

Grammar
Reflexive pronouns

1 Copy and complete 1–4 in the table with *himself*, *herself*, *themselves* and *ourselves*.

singular	
I	I treated **myself** to a new T-shirt.
you	Ask **yourself** these questions.
he	My brother earned (1) … £1,000.
she	My sister taught (2) … Italian.
it	This TV turns **itself** off.

plural	
we	We enjoyed (3) … at the party.
you	Did you behave **yourselves**?
they	They hurt (4) … in an accident.

ANALYSE
How do you use reflexive verbs in your language? Is the form different for each subject?

2 Match sentence beginnings 1–5 with endings a–e.

1 You could earn
2 David enjoyed
3 Babies can't look
4 Sandra saw
5 I didn't hurt

a) himself a lot.
b) myself.
c) yourself €100.
d) herself on TV.
e) after themselves.

3 Copy and complete the questions with the correct form of the verbs in brackets and a reflexive pronoun.

1 If you had €100, what would you … (treat) … to?
2 Where do young people go to … (enjoy) … in your town?
3 Have you ever … (hurt) … in an accident?
4 Do your classmates always … (behave) …?
5 Does your teacher ever … (talk to) …?
6 Have you ever … (teach) … a new skill?

4 Write answers to the questions in exercise 3 so they are true for you.

If I had €100, I would treat myself and buy some new clothes.

Grammar in context: Literature

5 Read the text and choose the correct answers. Then listen and check. 🔊 65

The Pearl
by John Steinbeck

CAN POSSESSIONS MAKE US HAPPY?

John Steinbeck (1902–1968) was an American writer (1) … other novels include *The Grapes of Wrath* and *Of Mice and Men*. In *The Pearl*, Steinbeck considers how we persuade (2) … that material possessions will make us happy. It's a story (3) … considers themes like greed and exploitation. This book was published in 1947, at a time (4) … life was very difficult for many working people.

The story is about a man called Kino (5) … finds a huge pearl. At first, he's very happy because he plans to sell the pearl for a lot of money. But then (6) … in the village finds out about the pearl, and life becomes very difficult for Kino and his wife Juana. But I'm not going to tell you (7) … that happens – you'll have to read it for (8) … !

	A	B	C
1	who	whose	which
2	us	myself	ourselves
3	where	that	who
4	which	when	where
5	who	which	whose
6	no one	someone	anyone
7	everywhere	everything	nothing
8	myself	itself	yourself

LITERATURE TASK
Find out more about John Steinbeck.
- Where was he born?
- When did he win the Nobel Prize for Literature?
- Who was Charley in Steinbeck's book *Travels with Charley*?

Charity adverts

LEARNING OUTCOME
✓ Use persuasion in a presentation

Today we're looking at the language of persuasion. We're preparing a group presentation to persuade people to support our charity fundraising.

TASK Use emotive language in a presentation

1. Read some adverts
2. Understand a team presentation
3. Write a presentation
4. Give a persuasive presentation

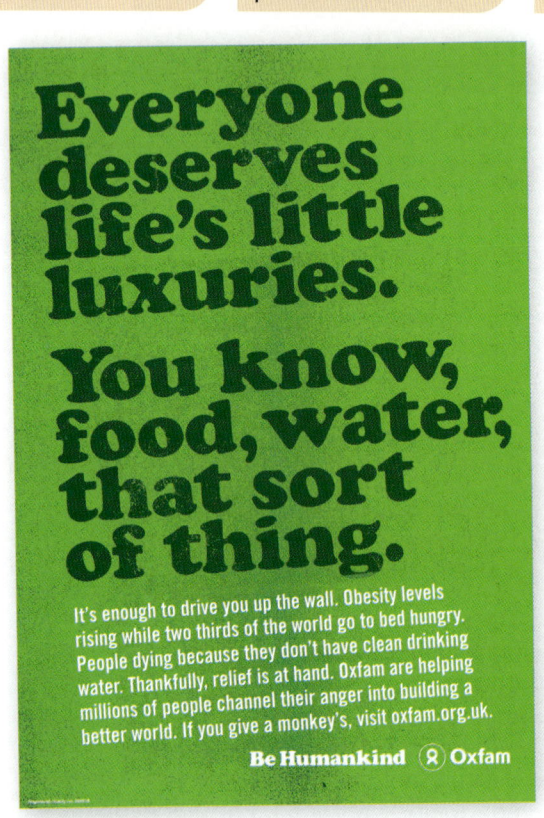

> Everyone deserves life's little luxuries. You know, food, water, that sort of thing.
>
> It's enough to drive you up the wall. Obesity levels rising while two thirds of the world go to bed hungry. People dying because they don't have clean drinking water. Thankfully, relief is at hand. Oxfam are helping millions of people channel their anger into building a better world. If you give a monkey's, visit oxfam.org.uk.
>
> **Be Humankind** Oxfam

> open up your eyes
>
> ~~CENSORED~~
> FACTS
> TRUTH
> FREE SPEECH
>
> The world needs open eyes and open mouths to defend freedom of speech and human rights.
>
> **Click here** to find out more.

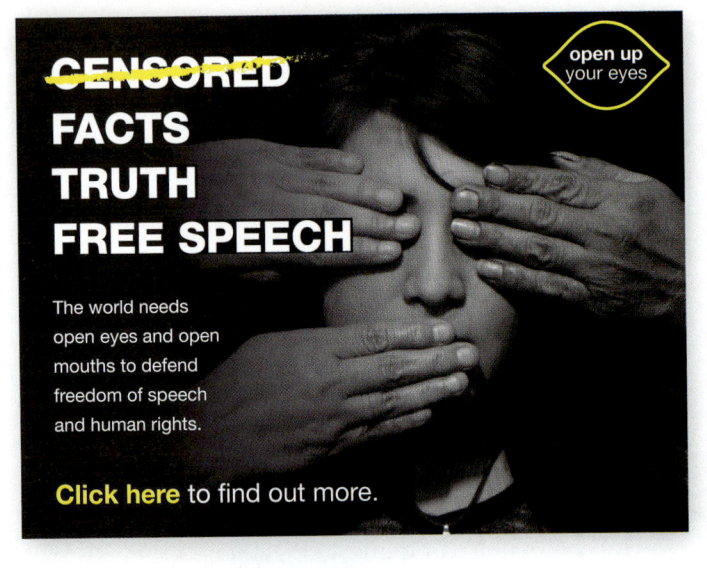

1 Read

1 Look at the adverts and answer the questions.
1. Which two charities have produced these adverts?
2. Which charity is fighting against censorship?
3. Which charity provides food and water to people in need?
4. How does each advert attract your attention? Think about:
   • colours   • design   • language
5. In your opinion, which advert is more persuasive? Why?

2 Read the adverts again. Find words or expressions that mean …
a) make you angry.
b) care about something.
c) the ability to say what you want.
d) the rights that everyone should have in a society.
e) when personal expression is not allowed for moral, religious or political reasons.

2 Listen

3 Read, watch or listen to the presentation on page 87. Complete 1–5 with five of these words. 🔊 66
  • £1   • 50p   • 90%   • 100%
  • agree   • disagree   • poverty
  • themselves   • yourselves

4 Watch or listen again Practise your intonation.

5 Listen to another presentation by Oliver and Jack. Choose the correct answers. 🔊 67
1. Oliver and Jack are selling **notebooks / socks / T-shirts**.
2. Amnesty International was set up in **1961 / 1981 / 1996**.
3. Amnesty has got about **300,000 / 3 million / 30 million** members.
4. Their product costs **£2.99 / £5.00 / £7.50**.

6 Look at the Communication kit on page 87. Which phrases are used in the Speaking sketch? Listen again to check your answers.

UNIT 8

SPEAKING SKETCH

Hello! We're Katy and Emily, and we're taking part in the Charity Fundraising Event this week. We're raising money for Oxfam – a charity which fights (1) … worldwide.

That's why we've made these delicious cupcakes to persuade you to part with your cash! Don't they look amazing? And they only cost (3) … each. Go on – treat (4) …!

All around the world there are people who have nothing to eat, and nowhere to get clean water. We're sure you'll (2) … that helping them is a fantastic cause.

We guarantee that (5) … of our profits will go directly to Oxfam. So, please buy a cupcake today, and help fight famine around the world!

Communication kit
- We're sure you'll agree that …
- Don't they look …?
- Go on – treat yourselves!
- We guarantee that …
- Please …
- You really should / ought to …

3 Write

7 Work in pairs. Decide and make notes about:
- the product which you're going to sell
- the charity which you're going to support

8 Prepare your presentation. Write two or three sentences for each of the four parts of the presentation.

about you ▸ about your charity ▸ about your product ▸ final summary

4 Communicate

9 In pairs, practise your presentation. Work together and divide the presentation between you equally. Try to make improvements.

💬 *Hello! We're Marta and Javier, and we're …*

10 Now listen to all the presentations. Whose is the most persuasive?

❗ COMMUNICATION TIP
EMOTIVE LANGUAGE

Use emotive language to persuade people to do or buy something. Emotive language causes people to feel a strong emotion, like excitement or hunger.

INTEGRATED SKILLS

Integrated skills ▸ Resource centre

87

Writing
A for and against essay

LEARNING OUTCOME
✔ Write a for and against essay about online advertising

---

debates online | HOME | DEBATES | OPINIONS | HEALTH

Should all adverts for unhealthy food be banned? 👍 Yes or 👎 No

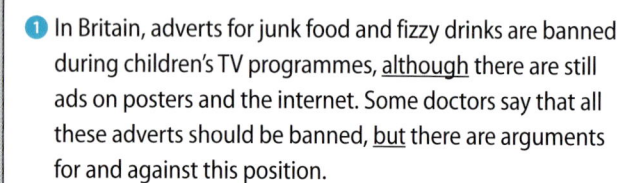

① In Britain, adverts for junk food and fizzy drinks are banned during children's TV programmes, <u>although</u> there are still ads on posters and the internet. Some doctors say that all these adverts should be banned, <u>but</u> there are arguments for and against this position.

② One of the main arguments for banning these adverts is that they are contributing to childhood obesity. Britain has got one of the highest rates of childhood obesity in Europe. <u>Furthermore</u>, adverts for other unhealthy habits (such as smoking) are already banned.

③ <u>On the other hand</u>, companies have the right to advertise their products in order to promote their business. <u>In addition</u>, perhaps it is the responsibility of consumers to make their own decisions about buying the products which are advertised.

④ To sum up, I am in favour of banning adverts for unhealthy food, <u>not only</u> on TV, <u>but also</u> on the internet. <u>Nevertheless</u>, it is also important to educate people to make good decisions about the food which they choose to eat.

---

1 Focus on content Read the essay and match paragraphs 1–4 with a–d.

  a) conclusion
  b) arguments against banning adverts
  c) introduction
  d) arguments for banning ads

2 Focus on language Read the information. Copy and complete the table with the <u>underlined</u> words from the text.

Connectors of addition and contrast

addition	contrast
Moreover, …	However, …
not only … but also …	

3 Choose the correct connectors.

  1 Online adverts are annoying, **but / moreover** they keep the content free.
  2 Pop-up ads are a distraction. **Furthermore / Nevertheless**, they can be sexist.
  3 On the one hand, online ads can be fun. **On the other hand / In addition**, they can waste time when you want to watch video clips.
  4 On the internet, **although you can / not only can you** get ads which are targeted at you, but you can also click on them immediately.

4 Write a for and against essay about online advertising.

Writing kit

1 Plan your essay. Which of these arguments are *for* online advertising and which are *against*? How many more arguments can you think of?

- Pop-up ads are really annoying.
- They keep the content free.
- You get ads which are targeted at you.

2 Write four paragraphs. Use the model essay to help you.
  1 introduce the topic
  2 advantages of online advertising
  3 disadvantages of online advertising
  4 conclude with your personal opinion

3 Useful phrases

There are arguments for and against this position
One of the main arguments for …
On the other hand, …
To sum up, …

4 Check your writing.

✓ connectors of addition and contrast
✓ vocabulary for advertising
✓ at least one relative pronoun
✓ four paragraphs

Study guide ▶ p106 | Writing hub ▶ Workbook p126

GET READY FOR YOUR EXAMS!

UNIT 9

LEARNING OUTCOMES IN THIS UNIT
- Review grammar, vocabulary and topics from the course
- Practise reading strategies
- Participate in a debate
- Write to an institution

VIDEO: GETTING STARTED
Watch the teenagers talking about exam preparation and answer the question.

Review quiz

1 Read the quiz and answer the questions. How much of New Pulse can you remember?

TEST YOURSELF!
How much do you remember from New Pulse 4?

1. Which rescue dog found 12 survivors in Mexico City?
   a) Bonny
   b) Little
   c) Frida
2. Who is Leah Mae Devine and what is her sister's name?
3. What does the acronym RNLI mean, and what does this organization do?
4. Young engineer Josh Mitchell won an award at 'The Big Bang' STEM fair. What kind of machine did he design?
5. True or false? More than 2 billion people around the world use a smartphone.
6. What's the name of the first James Bond Story?
7. In which country are the unusual rock formations of Cappadocia?
   a) Russia
   b) Turkey
   c) Peru
8. Give three examples of things that make up your digital footprint.
9. Which country is the young activist and blogger Hannah Alper from?
10. How fast does a Maglev train travel?  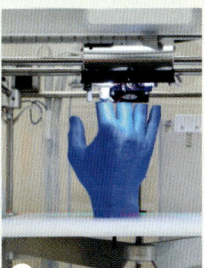    
11. Who opened the first car factories in the USA in 1908?
    a) Henry Ford
    b) Mercedes Benz
    c) Toyota Yaris
12. True or false? About 90,000 15–17-year-olds take part in NCS (National Citizen Service) in the UK every year.
13. With which rap star did Isaiah Acosta collaborate on the song *Oxygen to Fly*?
14. Which London underground station was taken over by cats for two weeks?
    a) Piccadilly Circus
    b) Baker Street
    c) Clapham Common
15. In which country was Matt Moniz climbing when an earthquake caused a huge avalanche?
16. What's the national minimum wage per hour for 16-year-olds in the UK?
17. Where does the Space Academy summer camp take place?
18. True or false? The World Wide Web was invented in 1999.
19. What does the acronym BFI mean, and what kind of courses do they organize?
20. Who wrote the comedy *A Midsummer Night's Dream*?

Vocabulary review
Revision

> **TIP!**
> During the course, you've learnt lots of new vocabulary. You've also studied different word-building techniques to expand your vocabulary. Review them regularly!

1 Match 1–6 with a–f.

1 reporting verbs
2 phrasal verbs
3 extreme adjectives
4 adverbs of degree
5 adverbs of manner
6 noun suffixes

a) endings (eg -*ness*) that are added to words to make new nouns
b) words that are stronger than normal adjectives
c) verbs that are used to report what someone said previously
d) words that tell us the intensity of something
e) a verb and a particle that have a different meaning together than the verb alone
f) words that modify a verb to tell us how something is done

2 Read the text and find …

1 a phrasal verb.
2 an extreme adjective.
3 a verb that collocates with 'university'.
4 one noun suffix.
5 at least two reporting verbs.
6 one regular and one irregular adverb of manner.

Reporting verbs

3 Choose the correct words.

1 Our teacher **promised** / **told** / **suggested** us to revise for a test tomorrow.
2 She **asked** / **refused** / **said** that we had to learn all the vocabulary.
3 We **complained** / **offered** / **convinced** that there wasn't enough time.
4 We **admitted** / **asked** / **said** her to give us time to revise.
5 She **suggested** / **agreed** / **invited** to postpone the test until Monday.
6 They **convinced** / **told** / **suggested** that we bring an extra pencil.

Phrasal verbs

4 Copy and complete the sentences with these words. There is one extra word.

• on • up • in • out • out • after • off

1 Look … yourself during the exam period. Make sure you eat and sleep well.
2 Meet … with the classmates you get … with best and study together.
3 Revising is hard work! Make sure you also allow time to hang … with your friends and family.
4 Don't go … the night before an exam.
5 Turn … your mobile during the exam.

Exams … what NOT to do!

A 52-year-old French woman posed as her 19-year-old daughter to take part of the Baccalaureat exam for her. The woman, identified as 'Caroline D', dressed in jeans and trainers, and wore make-up in an attempt to change her appearance. She managed to enter the exam hall and fill in her daughter's personal information on the examination paper. She then began the three-hour English exam.

Things were going well for the fraudster until an invigilator became suspicious. He alerted the police and quietly asked the woman to leave. She was taken to a police station, where she admitted that she had cheated and said that she only wanted to help her daughter.

The Baccalaureat is the final exam which French students must complete successfully before applying to university. Stress can be a huge problem for teenagers taking the 'Bac', and some parents are prepared to take desperate measures!

Adjectives and adverbs

5 Copy and complete the sentences with these words. Which one is an adjective? Are the other words adverbs of frequency, manner or degree?

- very
- absolutely
- terrifying
- rarely
- always

1 People … cheat in exams – it's too risky.
2 The exam didn't finish until 4pm. I was … starving at the end!
3 Exams can be … for people who suffer from exam phobia.
4 … read all the exam questions carefully before you try to answer them.
5 The test was … difficult – will I pass?

Easily confused words

6 Copy and complete the sentences with one word from each pair.

- wait / hope
- see / watch
- lend / borrow
- trip / voyage
- spend / waste

1 Plan your revision now. Don't … until the day before the exam!
2 It's useful to … revision guides from the library.
3 Don't … time. Stick to your study goals!
4 Take notes while you're revising. It's helpful to … the information in your own handwriting.
5 Enjoy your end-of-year … after the exams!

Noun suffixes

7 Copy and complete the table.

root word	noun with suffix
national (adj)	nationality
aware (adj)	(1) …
educate (v)	(2) …
employ (v)	(3) …
important (adj)	(4) …
citizen (n)	(5) …

8 Copy and complete the text with words in exercise 7.

To obtain citizenship in the UK, immigrants of another (1) *nationality* have to take an exam called 'Life in the UK'. Candidates must learn about British culture. For example, you must have an (2) … of the British (3) … system (schools and universities) and (4) … regulations (such as workers' rights). Knowledge of the English language is also very (5) … There are 24 questions, and you must answer 18 correctly. Then you can become a British (6) …!

TIP!
You can get apps to help you practise the pronunciation of new vocabulary. Try downloading 'Sounds: the Pronunciation app' to your smartphone or tablet.

9 Choose the correct words. Then listen and check. 68

Exam horrors

A monstrous mistake
A Level students at Newmarket College in Suffolk, England, were (1) **very / absolutely** horrified when they (2) **found out / gave up** that they had been taught the wrong book. Apparently, teachers weren't (3) **awareness / aware** that the exam text was *Frankenstein* not *Dracula*. Students received a five-hour intensive class days before the exam, and then (4) **waited / hoped** that the questions would be easy!

Singing socks
A student at Sheffield University was about to (5) **take / make** his final exam when he realized that he didn't have any clean socks to wear. Then he (6) **remembered / recorded** that he had received a pair of funny Rudolph socks for Christmas. The invigilator had to (7) **say / tell** him to take them off when they started playing the *Rudolph the Red-Nosed Reindeer* song half-way through the exam!

Pigeons cause chaos
Officials decided (8) **cancelling / to cancel** a final exam at Bangor University in Wales when pigeons flew into the exam room. Students (9) **complained / convinced** that it was impossible to concentrate because the birds were very (10) **noisy / noisily**. The university apologized to students and the exam was rescheduled.

Reading
A leaflet

LEARNING OUTCOME
✔ Practise reading strategies

> **TIP!**
> During the course, you've studied different strategies to improve your reading, and you've done many different types of comprehension activity. Keep practising these different techniques!

Reading strategies
Predicting content

1 Read the title of the text and look at the photo. Which three of these things do you think you'll read about?

- time management
- assertiveness
- healthy eating
- advertising
- taking exams
- identity theft

Skimming the text

2 Read the text quickly. Complete 1–4 with headings from a–e. There is one extra heading that you don't need.

a) How to stay healthy and beat exam nerves
b) How to revise
c) What to do during and after the exam
d) How to obtain sample papers
e) What to do the day before and the morning of your exam

Scanning for specific information

3 Read and listen to the text. Then find: 🔊 69

1 at least four things to help you revise
2 at least four ways of keeping healthy
3 three people you could ask for help
4 three things you should do the night before an exam

4 Words in context Find these words in the text. Then write definitions using *who*, *which* or *where* and the words in brackets.

A revision timetable is a plan which helps you to revise.

> revision timetable (plan)
> revision app (mobile application)
> sample papers (practice exams)
> gym (place)   counsellor (person)
> invigilator (person)

HOW TO ...
keep calm and pass exams!

Follow these tips before, during and after the exam.

Before the exam: revision and preparation

1 ...
Managing your time effectively is essential for good revision. Plan ahead – don't wait until the last minute! Make a revision timetable and find the revision techniques that work for you, varying the subjects so that you don't get bored. Online revision apps can be useful, but remember that people still used to pass exams before mobile phones were invented! So try turning off your phone to avoid getting distracted.

> *TOP TIP:*
> Find out exactly what type of activities will be in the exam, and do sample papers if possible.

2 ...
A healthy diet and plenty of sleep are essential to exam success. Instead of snacking on sweets, experts suggest bananas for a sustained energy boost. You'll lose concentration if you're dehydrated, so drink plenty of water – but avoid coffee because caffeine is no substitute for proper rest. You should aim to sleep eight to ten hours a night, and stop studying two hours before bedtime. Physical exercise is also important – not only does it improve concentration, but it also reduces stress. So keep a good study / life balance – you don't have to give up the gym or time with friends. Take regular breaks and use those activities as motivational 'treats'.

> *TOP TIP:*
> If you're feeling anxious about exams, ask a teacher, doctor or counsellor for help.

The longer read > Resource centre

Are you ready for exam day?

3 ...
Make sure you know exactly when the exam will be held, and find out how to get there if it isn't at your school. Prepare your bag the night before – you'll sleep better if you know that everything is ready. It goes without saying that you shouldn't go out the night before your exam, but neither should you stay up late revising! Try to switch off and have an early night, and set your alarm to avoid oversleeping.

> **TOP TIP:**
> Be sure to double-check the start time of your exam!

4 ...
When you're about to start the exam, read all the questions carefully and calculate how much time to dedicate to each section. If you don't understand the instructions, tell the invigilator straight away. After the exam, don't waste time comparing answers – it would be more effective if you had a good rest before preparing for your next exam.

> **TOP TIP:**
> Think positively and don't give up. Good luck!

Comprehension activities

5 Choose the correct answers. Find evidence in the text to support your choices.

1. Mobile phones …
   a) should be used in exams.
   b) are a good way of preparing for exams.
   c) can be a distraction during revision.
2. Caffeine …
   a) is not recommended.
   b) is a substitute for sleep.
   c) causes dehydration.
3. The night before an exam, you should …
   a) revise as much as possible.
   b) remember to set your alarm.
   c) go out with your friends.
4. After an exam you should …
   a) read the questions carefully.
   b) check the answers.
   c) have a rest.

6 Is the information true, false or not mentioned in the text?

1. It's a good idea to do sample papers before an exam.
2. Sweets are a good snack because they provide a sustained energy boost.
3. You shouldn't talk to your friends the night before an exam.
4. You should ask another student if you don't understand the instructions.

7 Answer the questions in your own words. Write full sentences.

1. Does the writer recommend using apps?
2. How much sleep should you try to get while you're doing exams?
3. What should you double-check the night before an exam?
4. What's the first thing you should do in an exam?

💡 CRITICAL THINKING

SUMMARIZE AND EVALUATE INFORMATION
Summarize the advice given in the text. Write a list of three important pieces of advice from each paragraph.
Evaluate the advice. Which four would *you* choose for the 'Top Tips'?

VIDEO: CULTURE BYTE
▶ Watch the video supplied by BBC.

Grammar
Revision

VIDEO: FLIPPED CLASSROOM
Watch the grammar presentation and do the task.

Review of grammar forms

1 Match questions 1–10 with grammar forms a–j. Then write answers. Remember to use the correct tenses and grammatical structures.

YOUR SCHOOL DAYS … HAPPY MEMORIES?

1 Which primary school did you use to go to before this school?
2 Had you already learnt to read before you started school?
3 Which year of your education have you enjoyed the most?
4 Were you ever told off by one of your teachers?
5 If you had had the opportunity to go to any school, where would you have gone?
6 Are you studying any subjects this year which you really enjoy?
7 If you could change one thing about your school, what would it be?
8 Do you think you might stay at this school next year?
9 When will you be taking your last obligatory exam?
10 Which of your teacher(s) will you always remember?

a) present continuous
b) present perfect
c) past perfect
d) used to
e) past passive
f) will / won't
g) future continuous
h) modals
i) second conditional
j) third conditional

2 In pairs, ask and answer the questions in exercise 1. Make notes using reported speech.

I asked Fatima which primary school she used to go to, and she told me …

Gerunds and infinitives

3 Complete the text with the infinitive with *to* or gerund form of the verbs in brackets.

HOW TO IMPROVE YOUR MEMORY!

A good memory depends on the health of your brain. Here are some things you can do (1) … (improve) your mental performance:

GIVE YOUR BRAIN A WORKOUT
Like muscles, you need (2) … (exercise) your brain! Do this by (3) … (learn) new things and getting out of your comfort zone.

BEAT STRESS
Did you know that chronic stress can destroy brain cells? Avoid stress if you want (4) … (keep) your brain healthy!

FUN AND LAUGHTER
(5) … (spend) time with friends has cognitive benefits. Did you know that laughter is good for the brain?

SUPERFOODS
Boost your brain power with plenty of fruit, vegetables and whole grains. Avoid (6) … (eat) too much sugar and saturated fat.

DEEP SLEEP
It's easier (7) … (remember) things after a good night's sleep. It's important (8) … (get) eight hours every night!

Conditionals

4 Copy and complete the sentences with the correct form of the verbs in brackets. Use the first, second or third conditional.

1 If you … (avoid) stress, your brain will be much healthier.
2 If I'd known that laughter is good for the brain, I … (spend) more time with my friends.
3 I … (sleep) better if I didn't have to get up so early in the morning.
4 I … (not fail) the test if I had revised more.
5 If I were you, I … (not worry) about it!

94 Grammar reference ▶ Workbook p100

Reported speech

5 Rewrite the sentences with reported speech. Change the tenses and the time expressions.

1 'I'm taking my English exam tomorrow.'
  Ana said that …
2 'I revised all the grammar yesterday.'
  She told me …
3 'I've forgotten what time the exam starts.'
  She admitted …
4 'I'm a bit nervous today.'
  She told me …
5 'I hope I'll pass.'
  She said that …

Verb tenses

6 Copy and complete the text with the correct form of the verbs in brackets.

What is memory?

Nowadays psychologists (1) … (describe) memory as the way the human brain obtains, stores and retrieves information. People (2) … (be) fascinated by memory for thousands of years. In fact, the study of memory (3) … (begin) more than 2,000 years ago, when the Greek philosopher Aristotle (4) … (write) his book *On Memory and Reminiscence*. But a scientific approach to memory (5) … (not exist) until the 1880s, when the psychologist Hermann Ebbinghaus (6) … (classify) the three types of memory: short-term, long-term and sensory memory. We still (7) … (use) this classification today. By the 1960s, computer scientists (8) … (begin) to compare the way memories are stored by humans and machines. If doctors and computer scientists work together, perhaps they (9) … (invent) a memory chip for humans in the future. Imagine that if you (10) … (have) an exam in a particular subject, you could simply insert the relevant memory card!

The passive

7 Rewrite the active sentences in the passive voice. Use *by* only when necessary.

The brain stores our memories.
Our memories are stored by the brain.

1 Psychologists study the process of memory.
2 Aristotle wrote *On Memory and Reminiscence*.
3 They improved computer memory in the 1980s.
4 Perhaps they will invent a memory chip for humans in the future.
5 A lot of students will use it!

CLIL Grammar in context: Literature

8 Read the text and choose the correct answers below.

Charles Dickens
(1812–1870)

Charles Dickens was an English writer (1) … novels are still popular today. He (2) … born in 1812. 12 years later, his father (3) … to prison because he couldn't (4) … his debts. Suddenly, Dickens (5) … to leave school and start working in a factory. He experienced terrible conditions, which he remembered all his life. Later, these experiences influenced his work. He probably (6) … have written novels such as *Oliver Twist* and *David Copperfield* if he hadn't experienced poverty (7) … . Dickens (8) … a successful journalist and a great philanthropist, campaigning for children's rights and social reform. By the time he died at the age of 58, Dickens (9) … 15 novels and hundreds of short stories. (10) … you read any of them yet?

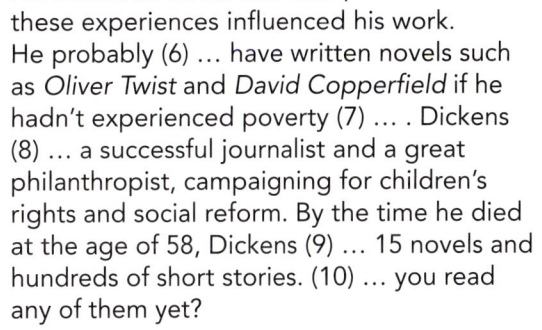

	A	B	C
1	who	whose	which
2	was	were	is
3	sent	was sent	were sent
4	pay	to pay	paid
5	must	had	didn't have
6	won't	would	wouldn't
7	herself	himself	themselves
8	became	has become	was becoming
9	wrote	has written	had written
10	Do	Have	Had

9 Listen and check your answers. 70

LITERATURE TASK

Choose one of these books, and write:
• a list of the main characters
• a short summary of the story

Oliver Twist   Great Expectations
A Tale of Two Cities   David Copperfield

Assessment methods

LEARNING OUTCOME
✓ Participate in a debate

Today we're going to debate whether exams are the best way to assess people. What do you think?

TASK Express your opinion

1. Read contrasting opinions
2. Identify opinions
3. Write a list of arguments
4. Participate in a debate

Home | Forums | GCSE | A Level | IB | University | Careers

ARE EXAMS THE BEST WAY TO ASSESS STUDENTS?

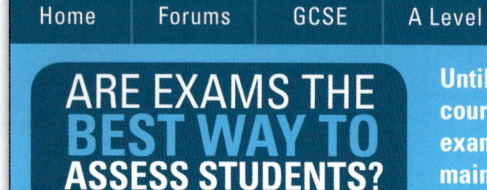

Until recently, most GCSE subjects in England were assessed by coursework throughout the year, or a combination of coursework and exams. But this is changing, and now most assessment for GCSEs is mainly by final exams only. Do you think this is a good idea?

50% SAY YES

I think that exams are the best kind of assessment, because they motivate you to work harder. Passing exams and getting good grades is an incentive like earning money when you have a job!
Posted by Amy

In my opinion, exams are the fairest assessment because you can't cheat. Someone else could do coursework for you, so it isn't a true test of your ability. But I also think we should be allowed to take reference materials into exams. In the real world, you can always check things online.
Posted by Brendan

The way I see it is that exams are the only really objective way to test people. It wouldn't be practical for teachers to assess everyone individually – it would take too long, and the teacher could be biased.
Posted by Caitlin

50% SAY NO

Exams are terrible for people who get stressed. It's not fair to judge someone's ability entirely on their performance in a single exam, is it? What if you're feeling ill or just having a bad day?
Posted by David

Everyone has different ways of learning, so there should be different ways of assessing people, too. Some people are more effective giving presentations, for example, or doing practical tasks or projects. I'm definitely in favour of continuous assessment throughout the course.
Posted by Eleanor

I don't think exams are a true test of knowledge and understanding. They only really test if you've got a good memory. When teachers just want you to pass exams, it makes school boring and limits creativity.
Posted by Freddie

---

1 Read

1 Read the text. Find words that mean …

1. schoolwork you do, where the mark is part of your final exam result.
2. numbers or letters that show the quality of a student's work.
3. to behave dishonestly in an exam.
4. giving someone special treatment.
5. all the facts you know about something.

2 Read the text again. Who thinks that …

1. you should be able to use books in exams?
2. some people are better at projects?
3. exams can be hard for people who get nervous?
4. exams are an incentive to study more?
5. exams only test whether you can memorize information?

2 Listen

3 Read, watch or listen to the extract from a group debate on page 97. Who is in favour of exams? 🔊 71

4 Watch or listen again. Practise your intonation.

5 Listen to the complete debate. Which three arguments are used in favour of exams? 🔊 72

1. Exams are fair because nobody can cheat.
2. Exams are like real life because you have to solve problems alone.
3. Preparing for exams helps you to understand what you've studied.
4. Preparing for exams helps to improve your memory.
5. Exams are objective when they're marked by an external assessor.

SPEAKING SKETCH

Teacher: OK, so, today we're going to discuss whether exams are the best way to assess students. Who would like to start the debate?

Jack: It's an interesting point, but it's not really true, is it? I mean, some people cheat in exams, don't they?

Oliver: I'm sorry, but I completely disagree. In my view, exams don't necessarily show that you've understood things. They just show that you can memorize lots of facts and information!

Emily: In my opinion, exams are the most effective type of assessment. I think the main argument is that exams are fairer because nobody can cheat.

Emily: Well, I suppose so, but not many, I don't think. Another argument is that preparing for exams helps you to learn. It makes sure that you understand everything you've studied during the year.

Communication kit
- In my opinion, …
- It's an interesting point, but …
- That's not really true, is it?
- Another argument is that …
- I'm sorry, but I completely disagree.

3 Write

6 Prepare your argument for the debate. Are you for or against exams? Write a list of arguments. Use the ideas on page 96 and your own ideas.

> **COMMUNICATION TIP**
> **REVISE AND PRACTISE**
>
> Periodically revise and practise communication strategies you learn during the course, such as giving opinions, agreeing and disagreeing and using question tags.

7 Look at the Communication kit. Find an example for 1–5.

1. using question tags
2. disagreeing with someone
3. sequencing your arguments
4. presenting your opinion
5. giving a counter-argument

4 Communicate

8 In pairs, prepare for the debate. Practise giving your opinions and agreeing or disagreeing.

💬 *In my opinion, …*
💬 *It's an interesting point, but …*

9 Have a class debate. At the end, have a class vote. Are the majority for or against exams?

INTEGRATED SKILLS

Integrated skills > Resource centre

Writing
Formal emails

LEARNING OUTCOME
✔ Write to an institution

Hi Oliver,

How are things? Hope your exams are going OK!

Here's that info I promised to send you about the grant to study abroad. You should definitely apply – you'll have an amazing time!

Good luck!

Paul

STUDY ABROAD PROGRAMME

Apply now!

Complete the online grant application and email it to Ms Travis at secretary@iba.eu

---

To: secretary@iba.eu
Subject: Grant application for 'Study Abroad Programme'

Dear Ms Travis,

Please find attached my completed application form for a grant from the Study Abroad Programme. As you will see, I am particularly interested in studying in Spain during the next academic year.

I am currently a student at Highton School in Newville. This year I am taking GCSE exams in nine subjects, and I am expected to pass with good grades. I have studied Spanish for four years and my level is B1. I went on a school exchange to Spain last year, so I already have some experience of living there.

I can assure you that I will make the most of this fantastic opportunity if I receive a grant to study abroad. After the Baccalaureate I hope to study modern languages at university, so it would be a great advantage if I could improve my language skills.

Thank you for considering my application. I look forward to hearing from you.

With best wishes,

Oliver Khan

---

1 Read Paul and Oliver's emails. Which is more formal?

2 **Focus on language** Write *formal* or *informal* for rules a–f.

Start with 'Hi' or 'Hello'. *informal*
a) Use exclamations.
b) Start with 'Dear …'.
c) Use contractions.
d) Use everyday expressions.
e) End with 'With best wishes'.
f) Ask personal questions.

3 **Focus on content** Read Oliver's email again. Find at least one example for 1–8.

1 present simple
2 present continuous
3 past simple
4 present perfect
5 present passive
6 future simple
7 first conditional
8 second conditional

TIP!
In a writing exam, you must show the examiner that you can use a variety of grammatical structures. Make a list (like the one in exercise 3) and try to include at least one example of each.

4 Imagine you're applying for a grant to study abroad. Write an email to send with your application form.

Writing kit

1 **Plan** your email. Answer these questions.
- Who are you writing to?
- What are you applying for?
- Where do you want to go? Have you been there before?
- What are you studying at the moment?
- What language skills have you got now?
- What are you planning to do in the future?

2 **Write** your email. Use the model email and the notes from your plan to help you.

3 **Check** your writing.

✔ use a variety of tenses and grammatical structures
✔ use formal language appropriately
✔ check your composition carefully

---

98 | Study guide ▶ p107 | Collaborative project 3 ▶ p112 | Writing hub ▶ Workbook p128

Study guide

UNIT 1

Grammar
Present perfect with *just*, *yet*, *already*, *for* and *since*

just

We've **just** baked cupcakes.
Anna has **just** learnt to ride a unicycle.

We use *just* with the present perfect to describe actions which happened very recently.

yet and already

Harry has **already** made a video blog.
He hasn't spoken in public **yet**.
Have you learnt first aid **yet**?

We use *already* with the present perfect to say that something has happened.
We use *yet* with the present perfect to talk about things we expect to happen.

for, since and How long …?

How long has Monica had a tablet?
She's had a tablet **for** four years.
(= a duration of time)
She's had a tablet **since** 2015.
(= a point in time)

We use *for* with the present perfect to describe a duration of time.
We use *since* with the present perfect to describe a point in time.
We use *How long …?* to ask a question about a duration of time.

Present perfect and past simple

present perfect

I**'ve studied** French for ten years.
I**'ve studied** French since I was six.

past simple

My mum **studied** Law when she was at university.

We use the present perfect for actions that began in the past and continue in the present.
We use the past simple for completed actions in the past.

Vocabulary
Skills and abilities

bake cupcakes
design a website
do magic tricks
edit photos
learn a foreign language
learn first aid
learn to juggle
make a video blog
perform on stage
play in a band
ride a unicycle
speak in public
write a song
write computer code

Life skills

active listening
assertiveness
conflict resolution
cooperation
creative thinking
entrepreneurship
money management
negotiation
problem-solving
respect for others
self-awareness
time management

Words in context

a.k.a.
assist
audience
blade
boost
fundraise
hiking
illusion
kick-start
levitate
out of (your) comfort zone

Word builder

assist – assistant
code – coder
dance – dancer
design – designer
illusion – illusionist
juggle – juggler
magic – magician
perform – performer
sing – singer

Speaking
Talking about skills and interests

I've had some experience of …
I'm really interested in …
For example, …
I'm good at … and …
People often say that I'm …
What I find most exciting about this opportunity is …

LEARNING OUTCOMES

Which symbol matches your progress for each section?

- Understand reference words
- Listen to a discussion for specific information
- Have an informal interview
- Write a blog post about a talent contest

Grammar reference > Workbook p84 Progress check > Workbook p14

Study guide

UNIT 2

Grammar
Past perfect and past simple

past perfect and past simple

The people had already escaped from the building when **the police arrived**.
Before **he went on the course**, **Tim hadn't written computer code before**.
Had the passengers put on their seatbelts before **the plane took off**?

We use the past perfect for actions that happened at a time in the past before the main event, which is usually expressed in the past simple.

Subject and object questions

subject questions

Paramedics give **first aid to patients**.
   subject   **object**
Who gives first aid?   **Paramedics**

object questions

The journalists interview **the plane crash survivors**.
   subject   **object**
Who do the journalists interview?
The plane crash survivors

Question words can be the subject or the object of the verb.
If the question word refers to the subject of the question, we don't use an auxiliary verb.
If the question word refers to the object of the question, we use an auxiliary verb (*do*, *does* or *did*).

Vocabulary
Rescue and survival

capsize
casualties
catch fire
crash
firefighters
give first aid
paramedics
receive compensation
search and rescue workers
send international aid
survivors
victims

Extreme adjectives

boiling
delighted
disgusting
exhausted
fascinating
freezing
furious
gorgeous
horrific
huge
starving
terrifying
tiny
unforgettable

Words in context

blister
bolt
damage
emergency services
equipment
flood
headset
navigation
run by
strike
stuck

Word builder

a drive-thru (US) = a drive-through restaurant (UK)
cab (US) = taxi (UK)
do the dishes (US) = wash up (UK)
elevator (US) = lift (UK)
movie (US) = film (UK)
smart (US) = clever (UK)
soccer (US) = football (UK)
start over (US) = start again (UK)
subway (US) = underground (UK)
vacation (US) = holiday (UK)

Speaking
Using question tags

That's the most important thing, **isn't it**?
I don't think we'll need it, **will we**?
It'll be boiling hot, **won't it**?
That isn't very useful, **is it**?
We could use that for (cooking), **couldn't we**?
We wouldn't use that, **would we**?

LEARNING OUTCOMES

Which symbol matches your progress for each section?

- Use topic sentences
- Listen to a news report for specific information
- Take part in a group discussion
- Write a news report about survival

Grammar reference > Workbook p86   Progress check > Workbook p22

Study guide

UNIT 3

Grammar
Future tenses

will / won't

I**'ll do** voluntary work.
You **won't have** any interviews.

be going to

Are you **going to study** abroad?

present continuous

Where **are** you **going** backpacking?

present simple

Buses **leave** at 11am.

might

Victoria **might get** a holiday job.

We use *will / won't* to talk about future predictions. We also use *will / won't* to talk about spontaneous promises, offers or decisions.
We use *be going to* for future intentions.
We use the present continuous for future arrangements.
We use the present simple for schedules and timetables.
We use *might* for future possibilities.

Future continuous

future continuous

I **will be applying** for a job in the UK in September.
I **won't be studying** during the holidays.
Where **will** you **be working** in three years' time?

We form the future continuous with *will / won't* + *be* + the *-ing* form of the verb.
We use the future continuous for actions that will be in progress at a specific time in the future.

Vocabulary
Future aspirations

apply for a job
do voluntary work
do work experience
get a degree
get a holiday job
go backpacking
go for an interview
go on an exchange
leave home
make money
make new friends
pass your driving test
pass your exams
study abroad

Time management

develop a routine
find a balance
get organized
make a list
meet a deadline
plan ahead
prioritize
put (something) off
set a goal
set a reminder
take a break
waste time

Words in context

Are you kidding?
Don't just take our word for it!
Exactly!
the best … in the world

Word builder

a paper round
find a balance
finish off
health and safety regulations
lift off
put (someone) off
set off
start off
switch off
take off
transferable skills

Speaking
Phrases for interviews

Pleased to meet you.
Please take a seat.
Thanks for coming in today.
We'll let you know our decision …
I look forward to hearing from you.
It's been a pleasure to meet you.

LEARNING OUTCOMES

Which symbol matches your progress for each section?

- Identify facts and opinions
- Listen to and make notes about a Q&A session
- Have a formal interview
- Write a CV for a work experience position

Grammar reference ▶ Workbook p88   Progress check ▶ Workbook p30

Study guide

UNIT 4

Grammar
The zero, first, second and third conditional

zero conditional

If / Unless + present simple ↔ present simple

If we**'re** happy, we **smile**.

first conditional

If / Unless + present simple ↔ *will / won't* + infinitive

If they **don't meet up** with us today, we**'ll meet** them tomorrow.

second conditional

If + past simple ↔ *would(n't)* + infinitive

If you **lived** in another country, which country **would** you **choose**?

third conditional

If + past perfect ↔ *would(n't)* + *have* + past participle

If I **hadn't fallen out** with my friend, we **would have gone** on holiday together.

We use the zero conditional for facts or things that are generally true.
We use the first conditional for possible or probable situations in the future.
We use the second conditional for hypothetical situations in the future.
We use the third conditional when we imagine the consequences of a situation after it has happened.

Adverbs of possibility and probability

Maybe the weather will be better in that country.

After I graduate from university, **perhaps** I will travel abroad.

If I were you, I would **probably** hang out with my friends tonight.

You **probably** shouldn't take photos here.

Maybe and *perhaps* go at the beginning of the sentence or clause.
Definitely and *probably* go after affirmative auxiliaries (*will*, *would*, etc) and forms of *be*.
Definitely and *probably* go before negative auxiliaries (*wouldn't*, *shouldn't*, etc) and forms of *be*.

Vocabulary
Phrasal verbs

ask out	look after
bring up	make up
fall out	meet up
get on	settle down
go out	split up
hang out	tell off

Non-verbal communication

frown	raise your eyebrows
gesticulate	roll your eyes
give (somebody) a hug	shake hands
hold hands	shrug your shoulders
kiss (somebody) on the cheek	smile
	stare
make eye contact	

Words in context

ambassador	keep an open mind
get distracted	live with
go viral	multi-task
interrupt	pitch
jaw	requirement
jump to conclusions	tone

Word builder

a dream come true
actions speak louder than words
to cut a long story short

Speaking
Presenting your opinion

Personally, I'd say that …
I think / don't think that …
If you ask me, …
In my opinion, …
In my view, …
For me, …

📓 LEARNING OUTCOMES

Which symbol matches your progress for each section?

- Take notes and summarize 😊 😐 ☹
- Listen to a radio phone-in for specific information 😊 😐 ☹
- Have a group debate 😊 😐 ☹
- Write an instant message conversation 😊 😐 ☹

102 Grammar reference ▸ Workbook p90 Progress check ▸ Workbook p38

Study guide

Grammar
The passive

present simple passive
- **+** New gadgets **are invented** every year.
- **-** Science fairs **aren't attended** by everyone.
- **?** Where **are** they **made**?

past simple passive
- **+** A product **was designed** by three teenagers.
- **-** Some types of plastic **weren't used**.
- **?** **Were** we **given** a prize?

future passive
- **+** New technologies **will be developed** soon.
- **-** Space travel **won't be introduced** this year.
- **?** **Will** other planets **be inhabited** by humans in the future?

We use the passive when we don't know who does the action, or if the action is more important than the person who does it.

Active and passive voice

active and passive voice

In the **active** voice, the subject of a sentence is active: it does something.

Scientists build **rockets**.
Rockets are built by **scientists**.

In the **passive** voice, the subject is passive: something is done to it.

We use *by* in passive sentences when we want to express who or what does the action.

Vocabulary
Innovation and invention

3D printing	high-speed trains
bioplastics	satellite broadband
desalinated water	smart materials
driverless cars	space station
e-reader	space tourism
flexible smartphones	wearable gadgets

Adverb review

absolutely	fast	safely
always	often	usually
comfortably	quickly	very
easily	quite	well
extremely	rarely	

Words in context

award	pick up
eye strain	pitch
fair	replace
headset	stand
nanotechnology	up-to-date

Word builder

ability – disability	logical – illogical
advantage – disadvantage	patient – impatient
effective – ineffective	rational – irrational
expensive – inexpensive	visible – invisible
likely – unlikely	

Speaking
Sequencing events

In the early / mid- / late (1970s), …
Then / Next / After that, …
The following year, …
It wasn't until (1985) that …
By (the mid-1990s), …
Later / (A few) years later, …

LEARNING OUTCOMES

Which symbol matches your progress for each section?
- Scan for names, numbers and abbreviations
- Understand technical instructions from a TV show
- Give a presentation
- Write a formal letter of complaint about a faulty product

Study guide

Grammar
Modals of ability and possibility, obligation and prohibition

present	past
ability and possibility	
+ In the UK you **can** get a part-time job when you're 13.	I **could** ride a bike when I was six.
- You **can't** get a bank loan until you're 18.	I **couldn't** skate.
obligation and prohibition	
+ You **must** / **have to** cancel your credit card if it is stolen.	When I was 12, I **had to** go to bed at nine o'clock.
- You **mustn't** open phishing emails.	
no obligation	
- You **don't have to have** an email account.	They **didn't have to go** to work.

We use *can* or *could* to talk about for ability and possibility.
We use *must* or *have to* to talk about obligation.
We use *don't have to* when there is no obligation or something isn't necessary.
We don't use *must* / *mustn't* in the past.

Modals of deduction

modals of deduction
She **can't be** at school today – she didn't come to class. She **must be** ill. This email looks suspicious. It **might be** a phishing email. I'm not going to open it. It **could be** risky.

We use *must* and *can't* when we are certain.
We use *might* or *could* when we think something is possible, but we aren't certain.

Vocabulary
Identity theft
bank account
credit card
credit rating
debt
fraudster
junk mail
loan

log on
phishing
scam
shred documents
social networking site
spending spree
wi-fi hotspot

Personal identity
appearance
beliefs
ethnicity
friendship
gender
nationality

peer group
personality
possession
relationship
style
values

Words in context
asset
fake news
harmful
inappropriate
lock
pretend

regret
reputation
rumours
screen-grab
strangers
throw away

Word builder
get online
get your hands on something

Speaking
Giving counter-arguments
I'm sorry, but I completely disagree.
I don't see it like that at all.
That's not how I see it.
I'm afraid I don't agree.
You've made some interesting points, but I see things differently.

LEARNING OUTCOMES
Which symbol matches your progress for each section?
- Identify text purpose
- Listen to a radio discussion for specific information
- Argue for and against something
- Write a profile of someone you admire

Study guide

Grammar
Reported speech

direct speech
'We **filmed** the movie in Greece,' said Chris.

reported speech
Chris said (that) they **had filmed** the movie in Greece.

In reported speech the tense changes from the one the speaker originally used.

tense changes	
direct speech →	reported speech
am / is / are	was / were
present simple	past simple
present continuous	past continuous
past simple	past perfect
present perfect	past perfect
will or would	would
must or have to	had to
can or could	could

Reported questions

wh- / how questions
'When **will** the premiere **be**?' a) We **asked** when the premiere **would be**. 'Where **are** we **going to listen** to the soundtrack?' b) We asked where we **were going to listen** to the soundtrack.

yes / no questions
'**Is** the director Italian?' c) He asked if / whether the director **was** Italian. 'Have you **met** the crew?' d) She asked if / whether I **had met** the crew.

We change the tenses in the same way as in reported speech, but the word order is the same as affirmative sentences.
We use *if* or *whether* to report *Yes / No* questions.

Vocabulary
Film-making

camera operator	make-up artist
cast	script
costume designer	set designer
credits	sound effects
crew	soundtrack
lighting	storyboard
location	subtitles

Reporting verbs

admit	convince	refuse
agree	invite	say
ask	offer	suggest
complain	promise	tell

Words in context

buff	props
e-sports	residential
hands-on	streaming
inseparable	subsidized
overwhelming	viewers

Word builder

committed to	interested in
excited about	involved in
happy with	well known for

Speaking
Phrases for surveys

I'm doing some research into …
Could I ask you a few questions?
It won't take longer than five minutes.
I'll be taking notes – is that OK?
OK, let's get started!
Could you tell me …
Would you mind me telling me …?
Is there anything else you'd like to add?

LEARNING OUTCOMES

Which symbol matches your progress for each section?
- Recognize informal language
- Listen to and understand phone calls and messages
- Inform your class about survey results
- Write a report

Study guide

Grammar
Relative pronouns

who, which, where, when, whose

She's a celebrity **who** / **that** wins a lot of awards.	
I read about an eye-catching advertising campaign **which** / **that** went viral.	
Evenings are usually **when** television audiences are at their highest.	
He's the director **whose** films make the most money at the box office.	
Los Angeles is the city **where** most American TV shows are filmed.	

We use relative pronouns to give extra information about people, places or things. We use relative pronouns after the noun they describe. We can use *that* instead of *who* or *which*.

Indefinite pronouns

some-, any-, no- compounds

School is **somewhere** where there are usually no adverts.
They can't find **anywhere** to advertise.
There's **nowhere** to relax at school.
Is there **anywhere** quiet to revise?

We usually use *some-* in affirmative sentences. We use *any-* in negative sentences and questions.
We use *no-* with an affirmative verb.

Reflexive pronouns

singular	
I	I bought **myself** a sandwich.
you	You must look after **yourself**!
he	He taught **himself** to swim.
she	My friend taught **herself** to ride a bike.
it	This smartphone turns **itself** off.

plural	
we	We didn't enjoy **ourselves** at the beach.
you	Did you bake the cakes **yourselves**?
they	They saw **themselves** on TV.

Vocabulary
Advertising

ad agency	go viral
advert	hype
advertising campaign	jingle
brand	online ads
celebrity	peer pressure
consumer	persuasive
eye-catching	target audience

Easily confused verbs

borrow / lend	see / watch
hope / wait	spend / waste
remember / remind	win / earn

Words in context

bargain	gender	supporter
billboard	infrastructure	swipe
bombard	mood	
catchy	raise (money)	

Word builder

get a reward	lend a hand
give (someone) a hand	receive a reward
have a break	take a break

Speaking
Phrases for persuading

We're sure you'll agree that …
Don't they look …?
Go on – treat yourselves!
We guarantee that …
Please …
You really should / ought to …

LEARNING OUTCOMES

Which symbol matches your progress for each section?
- Guess meaning from context
- Understand numbers and prices in radio adverts
- Use emotive language in a presentation
- Write a for and against essay about online advertising

Study guide

UNIT 9

Review Units 1–8

Grammar review
Grammatical forms review (Starter – Unit 8)
Gerunds and Infinitives (Starter p5)
Conditionals (Unit 4 p42)
Reported speech (Unit 7 p72)
Verb tenses (Starter – Unit 3)
The passive (Unit 5 p52)

Vocabulary review

Reporting verbs
admit
agree
ask
complain
convince
invite
offer
promise
refuse
say
suggest
tell

Phrasal verbs
get on
go out
hang out
meet up

Adjectives and adverbs
absolutely
always
rarely
terrifying
very

Easily confused words
lend / borrow
see / watch
spend / waste
trip / voyage
wait / hope

Noun suffixes
awareness
citizenship
education
employment
importance
nationality

Words in context
counsellor
gym
invigilator
revision app
revision timetable
sample papers

Speaking

Phrases for a debate
In my opinion, …
It's an interesting point, but …
That's not really true, is it?
Another argument is that …
I'm sorry, but I completely disagree.

LEARNING OUTCOMES

Which symbol matches your progress for each section?
- Practise reading strategies
- Participate in a debate
- Write to an institution
- Apply for a grant / scholarship

Grammar reference > Workbook p100   Progress check > Workbook p78

Giving a presentation

TASK Work in groups to give a presentation about an entrepreneur or an exciting new company.

1 Think — **2** Listen and plan — **3** Create — **4** Evaluate

1 Think

1 Look at the slides about *We Are Knitters* and answer the questions.

1. What different information is in the slides?
2. How is the information easy to follow?
3. Could you improve the presentation? How?

@ DIGITAL LITERACY

When you give a presentation:
DO
- include an overview, introduction and conclusion.
- practise giving the presentation.
- check the computer works properly.
- say you will answer questions at the end.

DON'T
- include too many slides – it's better to have a few clear slides.
- speak too fast or too quietly.
- talk for too long.

a) YOUNG ENTREPRENEURS
OVERVIEW
1. Introduction
2. *We Are Knitters* – What? Who? Why?
3. More about We Are Knitters
4. About the products
5. Conclusion

b) We Are Knitters

WHAT?
- a knitting and fashion brand

WHO?
- María José Marín and Alberto Bravo, two young Spanish entrepreneurs

WHY?
- knitting really popular with many trendy people in Paris, New York & Hollywood – even film stars knitting! – wanted to make this traditional art cool everywhere
- company teaches people of all ages to knit

c) More about *We Are Knitters*

- María José and Alberto worked extremely hard to make their business a success
- overcame many practical problems, eg move to a bigger office and change suppliers
- learnt new business skills – how to delegate and how to launch product in new markets such as the USA
- appeared in a TV series about new entrepreneurs

d) About the products

- all designs are for the latest fashions – buy a kit from the website
- kits have everything you need – easy-to-follow instructions, needles, wool, accessories, designs from beginner to advanced
- videos on the website help you with any problems
- lots of people post pictures on Instagram when they finish!

2 Read the slides again and answer the questions.

1. What kind of company is We Are Knitters?
2. Who started the company? Why?
3. What problems did they have to overcome?
4. What did they have to learn about?
5. What do the knitting kits include?

2 Listen and plan

3 Listen to Pablo, Gema and Luisa doing the task. In which order do they talk about these things? 🔊 73

a) speaking more slowly
b) using your own words
c) varying your tone of voice
d) reading what's on the slide
e) repeating key words
f) pausing after important information

4 Complete the conversation extract with the words in the box. Listen again and check your answers.

| exactly | more | own | pause | too | vary |

Luisa: Wait a minute! You're reading (1) … what's on the slide. That's really boring.
Pablo: I agree. And you're speaking too fast. I think it will help if you speak (2) … slowly. And you didn't pause once!
Gema: OK, good idea. I'll try and (3) … after important information, too.
Luisa: Perhaps you should use your (4) … words and then put up each point after you've talked about it.
Gema: Yes, I think that will help.
Pablo: Another idea might be to (5) … your voice tone. You could repeat some key words, too. We Are Knitters is one of Spain's most exciting new companies!
Gema: That sounds good. OK, so I could say: We Are Knitters is an exciting new company. This is definitely knitting for the 21st century! Two young Spanish entrepreneurs started the company.
Pablo: That's brilliant. Your voice is good and you're not speaking (6) … fast.
Luisa: Yes and you've made it sound interesting. You're using your own words. You sound great!

5 Work in groups. Plan and practise your presentation. Use the Useful language box to help you.

- Choose the person or company you are going to do the presentation about.
- Decide what information to include.
- Decide how to share the work.
- Decide who is responsible for presenting each section.

3 Create

6 Follow the steps to create your presentation.

Share information
Read and listen to each other's work. Check these things:
- Is it in your own words?
- Have you got all the information you need?
- Are the grammar and vocabulary correct?
- Can you improve it?

Create the presentation
Write slides A–D of the presentation. Add titles, headings, photos and video clips. Then, edit the presentation. Check the grammar and vocabulary again. Can you make the presentation more attractive?

Practise giving the presentation
Practise your sections and then listen to each other. What can you improve?

Show and tell
Give your presentation to the class.

4 Evaluate

7 Now ask your teacher for the group and individual assessment grids. Then complete the grids.

Useful language
What about (speaking more slowly)?
I think it will help if you (pause after important information).
Perhaps you should (point at the photo).
Another idea might be to (ask the audience a question).
You could (repeat the important information).

Developing an app

TASK Work in groups of three to develop a simple app. Prepare the app and a description of it.

1 Think — **2** Listen and plan — **3** Create — **4** Evaluate

1 Think

1 Look at the apps below. Find an app for someone who:
1. wants to practise a foreign language
2. wants to be more environmentally friendly
3. has decided to get fitter and do more exercise

@ DIGITAL LITERACY

When you develop an app, remember to:
- think about the target users (Who is going to use it? How?)
- think of a simple interesting idea (What will people use it for? When?)
- use software to develop your app

Reviews | Guides | Phones | TVs | Photography | Best deals | Search

TOP APP Reviews ★★★★★

a) L-Lingo
L-Lingo is a fun way to learn and practise a new language.
With this app you can also do lessons offline.

b) Energy Track
Are you concerned about the environment? **Energy Track** helps you reduce your carbon footprint by showing you information about the energy you use.

c) Fitgo
Fitgo records the exercise you do and encourages you to get fit through social networking. It includes simple exercise programmes to help you. It has a fantastic feature that shows local parks, cycle paths and walks.

---

2 Look at the apps and descriptions again. Answer the questions.
1. Have you used these apps or similar ones?
2. Which do you think is the most / least interesting and most / least useful? Why?
3. What kind of information is included in the descriptions?

2 Listen and plan

3 Listen to Pablo, Gema and Luisa doing the task. Choose the correct answers. 🔊 74

1. They decide to create an app …
   a) for organizing homework.
   b) to check the spelling of English words.
   c) to play a game.
2. They decide the app should be …
   a) original.
   b) complicated.
   c) simple.
3. Who is going to …
   a) draw the screen design?
   b) research programs to write apps?
   c) write the description of the app?

4 Complete the conversation extract with the words in the box. Listen again and check your answers.

> like   mean   about   agree   should
> best   right

Pablo: OK, so we have to decide what kind of app we want to produce and how we're going to do it.
Luisa: Let's do a game app, maybe a fantasy game. That would be the (1) … thing.
Pablo: I don't see it (2) … that at all. I think we (3) … do an app related to learning English.
Gema: That's a great idea, but we have to decide who is going to use it and what they're going to use it for. I (4) … , there are lots of things you can do related to learning a language.
Pablo: Gema's (5) … . I think it should be for secondary school students, because we know a lot about them.
Gema: What (6) … a spellchecker for English words? That's really useful.
Luisa: Yes, that would be really helpful.
Pablo: I (7) … , but I think it's too complicated! This is our first app, so we should do something simple.

5 Work in groups. Plan your app. Use the Useful language box to help you.

- Decide who the app is for.
- Decide what exactly the app will do.
- Decide how to share the work.
- Decide when to meet again to share your information.

3 Create

6 Follow the steps to create your app.

Share information
Read or listen to each other's work. Discuss your work. Check these things:
- Can you improve the design and content of your app? Is the description attractive and interesting?
- Are the grammar and vocabulary correct?
- Are the spelling and punctuation correct?

Create the app
Finalize your design and create your app. Test your app. Then check the grammar, punctuation and spelling again.

Show and tell
Show the rest of the class your app. Answer any questions.

4 Evaluate

7 Now ask your teacher for the group and individual assessment grids. Then complete the grids.

Useful language
Suggesting
Let's (develop a music app).
Why don't we (add some music)?
What about (an app for revising vocabulary)?
What about (including a photo)?
We should (write an app for students).
Agreeing / Disagreeing
I agree / don't agree.
(Pablo) is right …
Clarifying
I mean …

COLLABORATIVE PROJECT

PROJECT 2

Making an advert

TASK Work in groups of three to make a TV or radio advert for a T-shirt printing business.

1. Think
2. Listen and plan
3. Create
4. Evaluate

1 Think

1 Look at the storyboard and the script. What is this advert for?

@ DIGITAL LITERACY

When you make a TV or radio advert, remember to:
- watch and listen to adverts to get ideas for creating your own.
- organize your ideas and prepare a detailed script. If you make a TV advert, prepare a simple storyboard.
- pay attention to speed and pronunciation while you are recording the advert.

STORYBOARD

Scene 1 – Script

Time	Who / What	Script
0.00	Dramatic music, camera shots of dirty car	–
0.10	Chloe	My car is dirty, but I haven't got time to clean it. I've got to pick my manager up in an hour. What shall I do? I know! I'll take it to Teen Clean!

Scene 2 – Script

Time	Who / What	Script
0.45	Camera shots of Teen Clean team cleaning the car Narrator 1 (David) Narrator 2 (Maria)	At Teen Clean we clean your car so well it looks new. We have the best prices in town! You'll be glad you called Teen Clean!
1.15	Camera shots of very clean car Chloe	Yes, I'll see you in five minutes.

Scene 3 – Script

Time	Who / What	Script
1.20	Outside the restaurant in clean car Chloe Marta Chloe (thinking – voice over) Narrator 1 (David) Narrator 2 (Maria)	Hi, Marta! Hi, Chloe! Have you got a new car? It looks great! Yes, thanks to Teen Clean! Any time you need your car cleaned, call or text us on 07981 328823. Remember, with Teen Clean your car will be so clean everyone will think it's new! Phone us now on 07981 328823.

2 Look at the storyboard and script again and answer the questions.

1 What does the storyboard show? Why is it useful?
2 How is the script organized? How many people take part?
3 Which of these advertising techniques do they use?

> humour   repetition
> talking about the benefits of the service
> addressing the customer directly
> persuading   celebrity endorsement

2 Listen and plan

3 Listen to Pablo, Luisa and Gema doing the task. Are the sentences true or false? Correct the false sentences. 🔊 75

1 They decide to write as many ideas as possible and then discuss them all.
2 They don't discuss any silly ideas.
3 They discuss using colours in the advert.
4 They look at some tips for creativity.
5 They finish by choosing the best ideas.

4 Complete the conversation extract with the words in the box. Listen again and check.

> discuss   funny   opinion   me
> think   could

Luisa: Let's make a list of ideas. I (1) … we should dress up as different celebrities wearing T-shirts we have printed.
Pablo: That's silly!
Gema: Let's make a list of all our ideas first, including the ones that seem silly. Then we can (2) … them.
Pablo: Good idea. In my (3) …, colours are important in adverts. For example, red is for action and youth. Green is for health and blue is for trust and security.
Gema: That's really interesting. We (4) … use different coloured T-shirts with slogans related to those things.
Pablo: For (5) …, the most important thing is that it's (6) …. People remember funny adverts. Maybe we could have a dog in a T-shirt!
Gema: That could be cool.
Pablo: Yeah, it could be part of a colour theme.

5 Work in groups. Plan your advert. Use the Useful language box to help you.

- Decide what kind of advert you are going to make.
- Decide on the content of the advert and how you are going to make it.
- Decide what each person is going to do.

3 Create

6 Follow the steps to create your advert.

Share information
Read or listen to each other's work. Discuss your work. Check these things:
- Have you chosen the best content ideas for the advert?
- Are the sentences clear? Do they get the listener's attention?
- Can you use a wider variety of words?

Create the script and storyboard
Write the final script and add the times.
Find any music or sounds you need to make the advert.

Make the advert
Film or record the advert as many times as necessary.
Edit the video or audio. Add any sound effects and music. Add any titles, subtitles, graphics or special effects.

Show and tell
Broadcast your advert to the class.

4 Evaluate

7 Now ask your teacher for the group and individual assessment grids. Then complete the grids.

Useful language
For me, the most important thing is …
That could (work) / That won't (work) because …
Should we (use celebrity endorsement)? What do you think?
How should we (plan this)?
Let's (read these tips). / What about (reading the tips)?
We have to remember to (include some music).

PROJECT 3

COLLABORATIVE PROJECT

External exam trainer: Speaking

Your exam preparation

1 Read and listen to the Model exam. Which topics does Ana mention? 🔊 76

1 name
2 age
3 hobbies
4 places
5 likes / dislikes
6 family
7 pets

2 Read questions 1–5 in the Model exam. Which question is asking about hobbies and leisure activities?

3 Read Ana's answers to the questions. Are the sentences true or false?

1 Ana has more than one surname.
2 She is 16.
3 She lives in a flat outside of the city.
4 She lives with three members of her family and a pet.

ABOUT THE EXAM

Introducing yourself
The examiner asks you for personal information – for example, your name, age, hobbies, where you live and who you live with. This tests your ability to give information about yourself and to have a simple conversation.

✓ EXAM TIP: Answering *wh-* questions

When responding to *wh-*questions (questions that begin with *what, who, how,* etc) remember to give as much information as possible. Don't just give a one-word answer!

Do you live in this city?

Yes. ✗

Yes, I do. I live in a flat in the city centre. ✓

MODEL EXAM

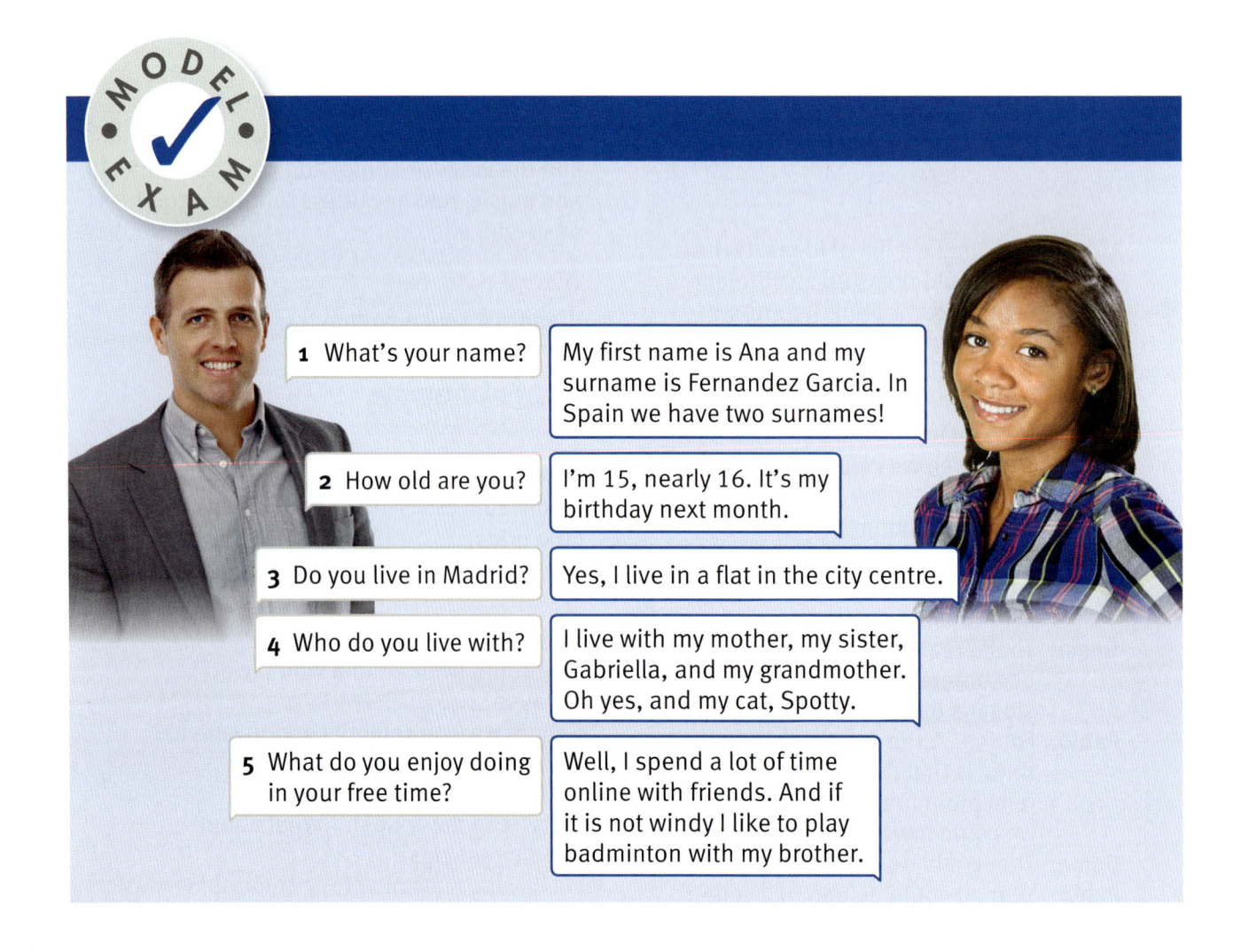

1 What's your name?
My first name is Ana and my surname is Fernandez Garcia. In Spain we have two surnames!

2 How old are you?
I'm 15, nearly 16. It's my birthday next month.

3 Do you live in Madrid?
Yes, I live in a flat in the city centre.

4 Who do you live with?
I live with my mother, my sister, Gabriella, and my grandmother. Oh yes, and my cat, Spotty.

5 What do you enjoy doing in your free time?
Well, I spend a lot of time online with friends. And if it is not windy I like to play badminton with my brother.

Introducing yourself

Your exam practice

4 Read questions 1–5 in Your exam. Match them with answers a–e.

a) I'm 16.
b) No, I live in Amsterdam.
c) I live with my mum and dad and my younger brother, Axel.
d) I like inventing and preparing new recipes.
e) My name's Peter. My last name is Jansen.

5 Add more information to the answers in exercise 4. You can invent the information!

a) I'm 16. It was my birthday last week.

> ✓ **EXAM TIP:** Give full answers to questions
>
> Try to give as much information as possible when you answer a question. Remember that you have to give true answers about your name and age, but you can invent answers for other questions. This can be useful if you cannot remember a word or phrase.

6 Answers questions 1–5 in Your exam with information that is true for you. Give as much information as possible.

7 Work in pairs. Ask and answer the questions in Your exam.

YOUR EXAM

1 What's your name? And your surname?
2 How old are you?
3 Do you live in this city? Where?
4 Who do you live with?
5 What do you enjoy doing in your free time?

✓ EXAM KIT: Useful language

Personal information
- My first name / surname is … • I'm (16).
- It's my birthday … • My birthday is on …
- next week • next month • the first / second, etc of January, February, etc

Where you live
- I'm from … • I live in … • I live with …
- a flat • a house

Family and pets
- mum • dad • sister • brother
- step-brother • step-sister • uncle • aunt
- grandmother • grandfather • cousin
- dog • cat • hamster • guinea pig
- gerbil • fish • reptile • turtle

Free time
- youth club • do magic tricks
- play in a band • do voluntary work
- make new friends

115

External exam trainer: Speaking

Your exam preparation

1 Work in pairs. Discuss which topics you think the examiner will ask about.

I'm sure they won't talk about school subjects.

- school subjects
- teachers
- places in your town
- friends
- family
- pets
- sport
- video games
- TV
- food
- holidays
- months of the year
- seasons
- health

2 Pietro is doing the Model exam. Listen and check your answers to exercise 1. Did any of the topics surprise you? 🔊 77

> ✓ **EXAM TIP:** Think about questions in advance
>
> Before the exam, think about the questions that the examiner might ask you and plan how you will answer them.

ABOUT THE EXAM

Talking about yourself
The examiner asks you questions about your daily life, your interests and the things you like. This tests your ability to have a conversation about the things that are important to you.

3 Listen to the conversation again. Complete the information about Pietro.

> **Likes:** French, the town (1) … , football, spaghetti with (2) … sauce, the month of (3) …
> **Sport:** PE at school (4) … a week, football training (5) … a week.
> **Holidays:** Different place every (6) … Last year (7), …
> **Best friend:** Gabriel, aged (8) … , good at maths and (9) …
> **TV:** Watches about (10) … hours per week.

4 Listen to Pietro's answers again. Which language for 'Giving yourself time to think' from the Exam kit on page 117 does Pietro use in his answers?

MODEL EXAM

1. Which school subject do you enjoy the most?

   Well, I think the subject that I enjoy the most is French. The teacher is really good and I'm learning so much.

2. Tell me about a place in your town that you really like.

   Let me think, somewhere in my town that I really like. I'd say the park. I often go there with my friends to play football.

3. How often do you do sport?

4. Where do you usually go on holiday?

   '…'

5. What's your favourite food?

6. Which month of the year do you like best and why?

7. Tell me about your best friend.

8. Over a week, how much time do you spend watching TV?

Talking about yourself

Your exam practice

5 Read questions 1–8 in Your exam. Match them with the beginnings of answers a–h.

a) Let's see. I do it every day of the week …
b) Let me think, somewhere in my country that I really like …
c) Well, that's a difficult question to answer because I like several different teams!
d) Well, I don't watch many videos, but I do watch …
e) I think the sport that I enjoy the most is …
f) Oh, that's an easy question for me to answer! I love Fridays because …
g) OK, so, my favourite aunt is called …
h) There isn't one place in particular that I go to.

6 Prepare your answers to the questions in Your exam. Make notes and use these things to help you:

- The beginnings of answers in exercise 5 where appropriate
- The Model exam on page 116
- The Useful language in the Exam kit

7 Work in pairs. Ask and answer the questions in Your exam. Remember to include extra information.

> ✓ **EXAM TIP:** Repetition
>
> If you didn't hear or understand the question, it's OK to ask the examiner or your partner to repeat it.
>
> *Sorry, can you repeat that, please?*

YOUR EXAM

1 Which sports do you enjoy the most?
2 Tell me about a city in your country that you really like.
3 How often do you do homework?
4 Where do you usually go at the weekend?
5 What's your favourite football team?
6 Which day of the week do you like best and why?
7 Tell me about your favourite aunt or uncle.
8 Over a week, how much time do you spend using a screen?

✓ EXAM KIT: Useful language

Giving yourself time to think
- Well, …   • Let me think …   • Let's see …
- That's a difficult question to answer because …
- Oh, that's an easy question for me to answer!
- OK, so …

Adverbs and expressions of frequency
- never   • rarely   • sometimes   • often
- usually   • always   • once / twice / three times a day / week / month / year

Likes and dislikes
- I (really) like / don't mind / enjoy / love / don't like / hate + noun / -ing
- My favourite / One of my favourite … is …

Describing people
- I've known him / her since …
- She's / He's good / brilliant / great at …

External exam trainer: Speaking

Your exam preparation

1 Look at the photos in the Model exam. Match sentences 1–4 with pictures A or B.

1 In the middle of the picture, I can see smoke coming out of the window.
2 In the foreground, there are two firefighters.
3 In the background, you can see the grey sky.
4 On the left, you can see flames coming out of the roof.

> ✓ **EXAM TIP:** Using narrative tenses
>
> When you describe past events, remember to use the past simple or past continuous after *at*, and the past perfect after *by*.
>
> *At six o'clock, I was watching the news.*
> *At seven o'clock, someone called the fire brigade.*
> *By eight o'clock, the firefighters had arrived.*

> **ABOUT THE EXAM**
> **Describing photos**
> The examiner will show you some photos, and ask you to describe them. This tests your range of vocabulary about different topics, and your ability to use narrative tenses to describe the photo effectively.

2 Read and listen to Jannik's Model exam. Answer the questions. 🔊 78

1 What was happening at 7pm?
2 What had happened by 8pm?

3 Read Jannik's Model exam again. How many examples can you find of:

- phrases from the Exam kit on page 119?
- verbs in the past perfect tense?

MODEL EXAM

Jannik

In these pictures I can see a building on fire. In the first picture, there's a building with smoke coming out of it. It's seven o'clock in the evening, and I hope that all the people managed to get out and call the fire brigade! By eight o'clock, the firefighters had arrived. In the second picture, I can see two firefighters in the foreground, with a fire hose. They're wearing helmets and protective clothing. In the background you can see the burning building, with flames coming out of the window.

A 7pm

B 8pm

Describing photos

Your exam practice

4 Look at photos A and B in Your exam. Which words from the Exam kit could you use to describe them?

5 Complete the sentences about the two photos.
1. In the foreground I can see …
2. In the background I can see …
3. In the middle there's …
4. At the top of the picture, you can see …

6 Prepare your description of photos A and B. Make notes and use these things to help you:
- the sentences in exercise 5
- the Model exam
- the Exam kit

☑ **EXAM TIP:** Organize your time

When you have to talk about more than one photo, make sure you organize your time effectively. Don't talk too much about one photo. Try to talk about each photo for the same amount of time.

7 Work in pairs. Cover your description and describe photos A and B. If possible, record yourselves!

A 10am

B 4pm

☑ **EXAM KIT:** Useful language

Rescue and survival
- boat
- branch
- building
- drive
- evacuate
- float
- flood
- flooded
- parked
- rescuers
- safe
- street
- victims
- windows

Describing photos
- In these pictures …
- In the first / second picture …
- In the foreground / middle / background …
- At the top / bottom …
- On the left / right …

Narrating events
- At … o'clock, (+ past simple or continuous)
- By … o'clock, (+ past perfect)

External exam trainer: Speaking

Your exam preparation

1 Read the instructions for the Model exam. Are sentences 1–3 true or false? Correct the false sentences.

  1 You're going to do the activity with the examiner.
  2 You don't have to reach an agreement.
  3 You have to give reasons for your choices.

2 Read the information in the Model exam. Who do you think would make the best exchange partners for Javier and Inés? Why?

3 Sophia and João are doing the activity. Read and listen to their dialogue. Is their choice the same or different from yours? 🔊 79

ABOUT THE EXAM
Collaborative task
The examiner will explain an activity to you and your partner. He / She will give you some information, and ask you to try to reach an agreement together. This tests your ability to cooperate and express your opinions.

✓ EXAM TIP: Reaching an agreement
You can agree and disagree with your partner during the discussion, but you must try to reach an agreement in the end. It doesn't matter if it isn't your true opinion! Don't forget to give reasons for your choices.

4 Read the dialogue again. Which phrases in the Exam kit on page 121 do Sophia and João use?

MODEL EXAM

Examiner's instructions
Javier and Inés are going on an exchange trip to Ireland. Read the information, then talk with your partner about which exchange partner you think they would get on best with. Try to reach an agreement, and give reasons for your choices.

JAVIER (16)
Family: 2 brothers, 1 sister
Likes: sports, music, camping

CHRIS (16)
Family: only child, pet dog
Likes: cinema, reading, art
OR
DAN (15)
Family: 2 sisters
Likes: concerts, football, Scouts

INÉS (15)
Family: 1 brother
Likes: photography, drawing, hanging out with friends

SALLY (16)
Family: 1 sister, a pet cat
Likes: music, web design, galleries
OR
EMMA (15)
Family: 2 brothers, 1 sister
Likes: volleyball, swimming, skating

João: What do you think, Sophia? Who would Javier get on best with?

Sophia: I'm not sure. Perhaps he'd get on well with Chris, because they're the same age.

João: I don't think so. Chris isn't into sport. I wonder if Javier would have more in common with Dan?

Sophia: Dan? Yes, perhaps. They're both into sport and music. I think he'd be the best exchange partner.

João: Yes, I agree. And what about Inés?

Sophia: I think Sally would be the best choice. She seems to be quite creative, too, so they'd probably get on well.

João: Yes, Emma is more sporty. I think Inés and Sally would enjoy hanging out together.

Collaborative task

Your exam practice

5 Read the instructions in Your exam. What are you preparing?

6 Look at pictures A–G in Your exam. Why are these things important? Can you think of any more things that are important to consider?

- health
- water cycle
- weather

7 Look at options A–G again. What's your opinion? Give a reason.

I think that … is the most important idea because …

☑ **EXAM TIP: Involve your partner**
Remember to build a conversation with your partner. Ask questions to get their opinion and listen carefully to their replies. This can give you more ideas to use.

8 Work in pairs. Discuss Your exam. Use these things to help you:
- your notes in exercises 5 and 6
- the Model exam on page 120
- the Useful language in the Exam kit

YOUR EXAM

Examiner's instructions
You and a classmate are preparing a presentation on the importance of water in our life. Talk together about the different uses of water and decide which ones you should include in your presentation.

H_2O

A, B, C, D, E, F, G

☑ **EXAM KIT: Useful language**

Talking about the uses of water
- drinking water
- extinguish fire
- ferryboat
- firehose
- have a shower
- hygiene
- mop and bucket
- transport
- water sports

Asking for opinions
- Do you agree with me?
- What's your view?
- What do you think?
- Are you OK with that?

Agreeing
- Yes, you're right
- That's a good point.
- Absolutely!
- Yes, I agree!

Disagreeing
- No, I don't think so.
- Absolutely not!
- I totally disagree.
- I'm not so sure about that.
- That's a nice idea, but …

External exam trainer: Speaking

Your exam preparation

1. Read and listen to the Model exam below. Do the candidates discuss the topic only with the examiner or with each other as well? 🔊 80

2. Read and listen to the Model exam again. Answer the questions.
   1. Why would Amy like to go on an exchange trip abroad?
   2. What does Ben say about his sister's experience of an exchange trip?
   3. Who does Ben get on best with in his family and why?
   4. Who does Amy get on best with in her family and why?

3. Which language in the Exam kit on page 123 do Amy and Ben use?

ABOUT THE EXAM
Discussing a topic
The examiner asks you questions related to the subject of the collaborative task which you will discuss with the examiner and / or your partner. This tests your ability to express your opinion and talk about your likes, dislikes, preferences and habits.

✓ EXAM TIP: Using personal experiences
As well as giving personal opinions, give examples of your own personal experiences of the topic being discussed, or those of friends and family members.

My older sister went …
For me, I think it would be …

MODEL EXAM

Examiner's question 1
Would you like to go on an exchange trip to another country?

Amy: Yes, I'd love to if I had the chance. I think it would be really interesting to spend some time abroad staying with a family and experiencing a different culture. What about you, Ben?

Ben: Yes, I completely agree. My older sister went on an exchange trip to Denmark a couple of years ago and she had a great time. She still keeps in touch with the family there. Do you think your school will organize an exchange trip in the future?

Amy: Well, actually, they are planning one with a school in France next year, but there are a limited number of places. I really hope I can go!

Examiner's question 2
Who do you get on best with in your family?

Ben: Let's see. I think I get on pretty well with all of them, but if I had to choose, I'd say my sister. Neither of us are into sport and we're both quite creative. We enjoy hanging out together and doing things like drawing and photography. How about you, Amy?

Amy: Well, for me, I think it would be my mum, actually. I get on OK with my brothers, but, to be honest, I've got more in common with my mum. We both like skating, for example, and we both love cats!

Discussing a topic

Your exam practice

4 Read the examiner's questions in Your exam below. What is the topic they are discussing?

5 Read the examiner's questions again. Which is the easiest question to answer, in your opinion? Which is the most difficult?

6 Work in pairs. Choose two questions from Your exam to ask each other. Think about your answers to the questions and make notes.

7 Ask and answer two questions from Your exam.

Use these things to help you:
- your notes in exercise 6
- the Model exam on page 122
- the Useful language in the Exam kit

✓ EXAM TIP: Cooperation

To be successful in the exam, you must communicate well with the examiner and with your partner. Remember to ask questions and respond to what your partner says. Don't show off, talk all the time or interrupt your partner!

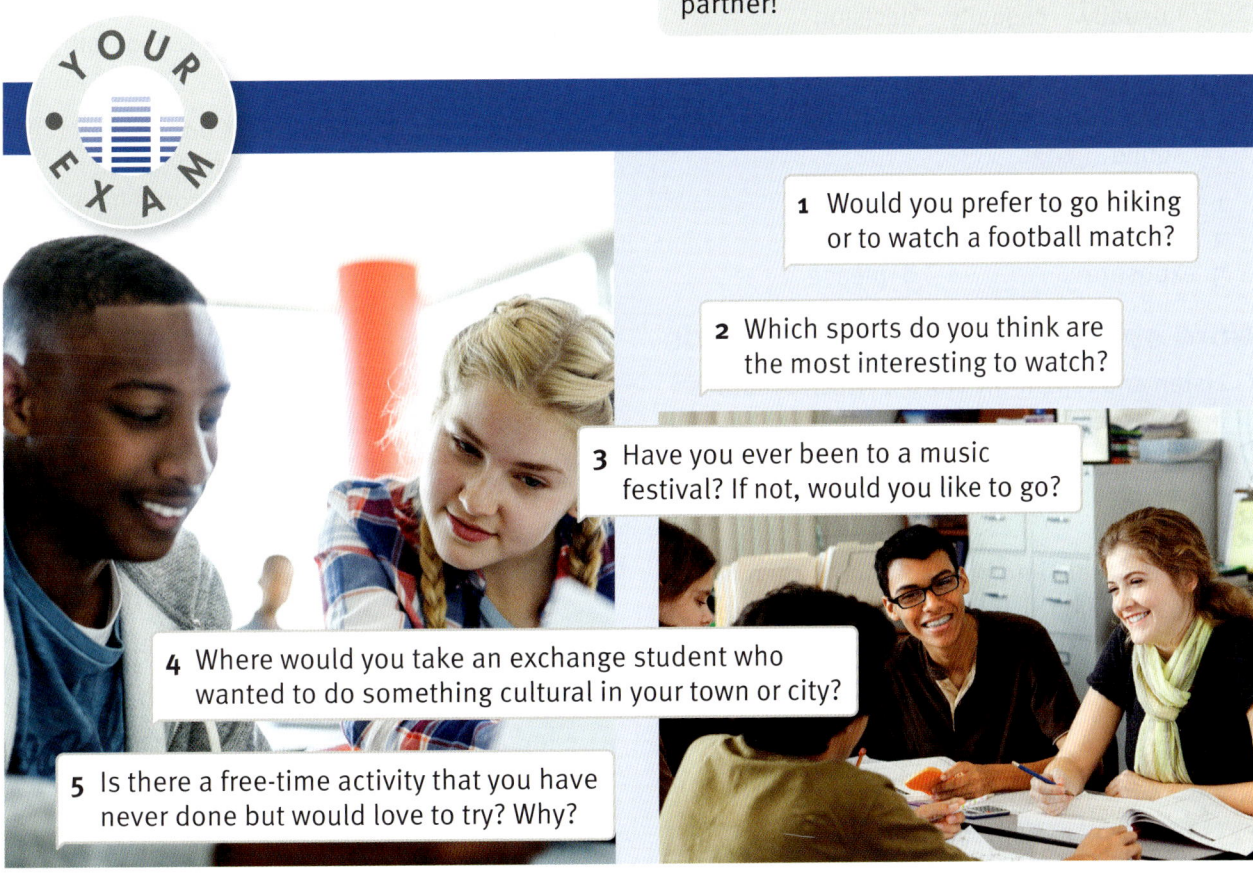

YOUR EXAM

1 Would you prefer to go hiking or to watch a football match?

2 Which sports do you think are the most interesting to watch?

3 Have you ever been to a music festival? If not, would you like to go?

4 Where would you take an exchange student who wanted to do something cultural in your town or city?

5 Is there a free-time activity that you have never done but would love to try? Why?

✓ EXAM KIT: Useful language

Free-time activities
- go hiking
- get to know each other
- get to know the area
- do something cultural
- go to an art gallery
- go to a music festival
- have a great time
- watch a football match

Adjectives
- beautiful
- boring
- fun
- interesting
- noisy
- quiet
- sunny
- wet

Giving opinions
- I think …
- I'd say …
- In my opinion, …
- For me …

Asking your partner's opinion
- What / How about you?
- Do you think …?
- Would you agree?

Talking about likes, dislikes and preferences
- I / We (both) love …
- I / We enjoy …
- I'm / We're (not) into …
- I'm / We're (not) keen on …
- I (really) don't like …
- I / I'd prefer … to …

123

Pronunciation lab

UNIT 1

-tion endings

1 Listen and repeat the words. 🔊 81

- resolution • cooperation • negotiation
- solution

2 Listen and write the words you hear. Practise your pronunciation. 🔊 82

UNIT 2

Difficult sounds: /ʒ/ and /z/

1 Listen and repeat the words. 🔊 83

| /ʒ/ | usually | casualty | decision |
| /z/ | victims | capsize | disasters |

2 Listen to the words. Which three have got the /ʒ/ sound? 🔊 84

1. television
2. zero
3. exposure
4. music
5. revision
6. please

Word stress in multi-syllable words

1 Listen and repeat the words. Which syllables are stressed? 🔊 85

gor•geous   hor•rif•ic   ab•so•lute•ly
starv•ing   fu•ri•ous   hil•ar•i•ous

2 Copy the table into your notebook. Then listen and complete the table with the words you hear. Which syllables are stressed? 🔊 86

2 syllables	3 syllables	4 syllables
freez•ing		

UNIT 3

Contractions: 'll and won't

1 Listen and repeat the short and full forms. 🔊 87

1. I will be going = I'll be going
2. He will not be studying = He won't be studying
3. What will you be doing? = What'll you be doing?

2 Listen and write the sentences. Do you hear the full or contracted forms? Practise your pronunciation. 🔊 88

UNIT 4

Intonation in conditional sentences

1 Listen and repeat. Pay attention to the intonation. 🔊 89

1. If you do your homework (↗), the teacher won't tell you off (↘).
2. If I were you (↗), I'd do it now (↘).
3. If I'd had time (↗), I would've done it (↘).

2 Copy the sentences into your notebook. Then listen. Does the intonation rise (↗) or fall (↘)? 🔊 90

1. I'll help you ( ) if you don't understand ( )!
2. I wouldn't do that ( ) if I were you ( ).
3. If I'd had your number ( ), I would have called you ( ).

Diphthongs

1 Copy the table into your notebook. Then listen and repeat the words. Pay attention to the pronunciation. 🔊 91

/aɪ/	/au/	/ea/	/eɪ/
smile	frown	stare	make
bite	out	hair	raise

2 Add these words to the table in exercise 1. Then listen, check and repeat. 🔊 92

- my • their • say • brown • care
- shake • fine • thousand

UNIT 5

Linking words: Final consonant + vowel sound

1 Listen and repeat. Pay attention to the linking (‿) between the final consonant and the following vowel sound. 🔊 93

1. He was‿awarded the science prize.
2. How‿are the designs going to be improved?
3. She is‿often late.
4. When is‿the competition taking place?

Pronunciation lab

2 Copy the sentences into your notebook. Listen and draw the linking (‿) where you hear it. 🔊 94

1. What are you designing?
2. I don't know anyone who's eaten at that restaurant.
3. I think this was invented by a German company.
4. How often do you watch television?

UNIT 6

/ə/ in *have to* / *had to*

1 Listen and repeat. Pay attention to the /ə/ sound at the end. 🔊 95

1. have to
2. has to
3. had to
4. didn't have to

2 Listen and repeat the sentences. 🔊 96

1. Do you have to be 18 to open a bank account?
2. You have to be careful when you use a wi-fi hotspot.
3. The fraudsters had to go to prison.

Silent letters

1 Listen and repeat the words. Pay attention to the silent letters. 🔊 97

1. debt
2. Wednesday
3. different
4. knife
5. half
6. government

2 Copy the words into your notebook. Then listen and underline the silent letters. 🔊 98

1. sandwich
2. would
3. thumb
4. autumn
5. vegetable
6. knee

UNIT 7

Intonation in reported speech

1 Listen and repeat the sentences in direct speech. Pay attention to the stressed words. 🔊 99

1. 'We've arrived at the festival.'
2. 'It's amazing!'
3. 'I hope it won't rain.'

2 Copy the reported speech into your notebook. Listen and underline the stressed words. Are they the same as the direct speech or different? 🔊 100

1. They said they'd arrived at the festival.
2. She said it was amazing.
3. He hoped it wouldn't rain.

UNIT 8

Difficult sounds: /s/ + consonant

1 Listen and repeat. Pay attention to the pronunciation at the beginning of the words. 🔊 101

- slogan
- start
- school
- spend
- square
- spread

2 Listen. Practise saying the sentence. 🔊 102

Students in Spain speak Spanish.

Difficult sounds: /ð/ and /θ/

1 We can pronounce 'th' in two different ways. Copy the table into your notebook. Then listen and repeat the words. 🔊 103

/ð/	/θ/
this they with	thing nothing Thursday

2 Add these words to the table in exercise 1. Then listen, check and repeat. 🔊 104

- the
- something
- that
- think
- other
- everything

125

Irregular verbs

Infinitive	Past simple	Past participle
be /biː/	was / were /wɒz/, /wɜː(r)/	been /biːn/
become /bɪˈkʌm/	became /bɪˈkeɪm/	become /bɪˈkʌm/
begin /bɪˈgɪn/	began /bɪˈgæn/	begun /bɪˈgʌn/
bet /bet/	bet /bet/	bet /bet/
break /breɪk/	broke /brəʊk/	broken /ˈbrəʊkən/
bring /brɪŋ/	brought /brɔːt/	brought /brɔːt/
broadcast /ˈbrɔːdˌkɑːst/	broadcast /ˈbrɔːdˌkɑːst/	broadcast /ˈbrɔːdˌkɑːst/
build /bɪld/	built /bɪlt/	built /bɪlt/
burn /bɪld/	burnt / burned /bɜː(r)nt/, /bɜː(r)nd/	burnt / burned /bɜː(r)nt/, /bɜː(r)nd/
buy /baɪ/	bought /bɔːt/	bought /bɔːt/
catch /kætʃ/	caught /kɔːt/	caught /kɔːt/
choose /tʃuːz/	chose /tʃəʊz/	chosen /ˈtʃəʊz(ə)n/
come /kʌm/	came /keɪm/	come /kʌm/
do /duː/	did /dɪd/	done /dʌn/
drink /drɪŋk/	drank /dræŋk/	drunk /drʌŋk/
drive /draɪv/	drove /drəʊv/	driven /ˈdrɪv(ə)n/
eat /iːt/	ate /eɪt/	eaten /ˈiːt(ə)n/
fall /fɔːl/	fell /fel/	fallen /ˈfɔːlən/
feed /fiːd/	fed /fed/	fed /fed/
feel /fiːl/	felt /felt/	felt /felt/
fight /faɪt/	fought /fɔːt/	fought /fɔːt/
find /faɪnd/	found /faʊnd/	found /faʊnd/
fly /flaɪ/	flew /fluː/	flown /fləʊn/
forget /fə(r)ˈget/	forgot /fə(r)ˈgɒt/	forgotten /fə(r)ˈgɒt(ə)n/
get /get/	got /gɒt/	got /gɒt/
give /gɪv/	gave /geɪv/	given /ˈgɪv(ə)n/
go /gəʊ/	went /went/	gone /gɒn/
grow /grəʊ/	grew /gruː/	grown /grəʊn/
have /hæv/	had /hæd/	had /hæd/
hear /hɪə(r)/	heard /hɜː(r)d/	heard /hɜː(r)d/
hide /haɪd/	hid /hɪd/	hidden /ˈhɪd(ə)n/
hit /hɪt/	hit /hɪt/	hit /hɪt/
know /nəʊ/	knew /njuː/	known /nəʊn/
learn /lɜː(r)n/	learnt / learned /lɜː(r)nt/, /lɜː(r)nd/	learnt / learned /lɜː(r)nt/, /lɜː(r)nd/
leave /liːv/	left /left/	left /left/
let /let/	let /let/	let /let/
lose /luːz/	lost /lɒst/	lost /lɒst/
make /meɪk/	made /meɪd/	made /meɪd/
mean /miːn/	meant /ment/	meant /ment/

meet /miːt/	met /met/	met /met/
pay /peɪ/	paid /peɪd/	paid /peɪd/
put /pʊt/	put /pʊt/	put /pʊt/
read /riːd/	read /red/	read /red/
ride /raɪd/	rode /rəʊd/	ridden /ˈrɪd(ə)n/
rise /raɪz/	rose /rəʊz/	risen /ˈrɪz(ə)n/
run /rʌn/	ran /ræn/	run /rʌn/
say /seɪ/	said /sed/	said /sed/
see /siː/	saw /sɔː/	seen /siːn/
sell /sel/	sold /səʊld/	sold /səʊld/
sing /sɪŋ/	sang /sæŋ/	sung /sʌŋ/
sit /sɪt/	sat /sæt/	sat /sæt/
sleep /sliːp/	slept /slept/	slept /slept/
speak /spiːk/	spoke /spəʊk/	spoken /ˈspəʊkən/
spend /spend/	spent /spent/	spent /spent/
stand /stænd/	stood /stʊd/	stood /stʊd/
steal /stiːl/	stole /stəʊl/	stolen /ˈstəʊlən/
take /teɪk/	took /tʊk/	taken /ˈteɪkən/
teach /tiːtʃ/	taught /tɔːt/	taught /tɔːt/
tell /tel/	told /təʊld/	told /təʊld/
think /θɪŋk/	thought /θɔːt/	thought /θɔːt/
throw /θrəʊ/	threw /θruː/	thrown /θrəʊn/
understand /ʌndə(r)ˈstænd/	understood /ʌndə(r)ˈstʊd/	understood /ʌndə(r)ˈstʊd/
wake /weɪk/	woke /wəʊk/	woken /ˈwəʊkən/
wear /weə(r)/	wore /wɔː(r)/	worn /wɔː(r)n/
win /wɪn/	won /wʌn/	won /wʌn/
write /raɪt/	wrote /rəʊt/	written /ˈrɪt(ə)n/

See full list of irregular verbs in New Pulse Workbook 4 > pp 158–160

Citations

p14 – Fact from National Citizen Service Trust, 2019.
p34 – Fact from Gov.UK, Crown copyright, 2018.
p44 – Fact from *The College Administrator's Survival Guide* by C. K. Gunsalus, Harvard University Press, 2006.
p44 – Data from What Next Consultancy, What Next Consultancy Limited, 2019.
p61 – Data from Comparitech, 2018.
p64 – Fact from Australian Communications and Media Authority, 2013.
p74 – Statistic from Mobile Marketing Magazine online, 2017.
p74 – Data from Global Music Report 2017, IFPI, 2017.
p74 – Data from We Are Happy Media PTY Limited, 2017.
p74 – Data from Essential Facts about the Computer and Video Game Industry Report, Entertainment Software Association, 2015.
p74 – Data from Big Fish Games, Inc, 2017.
p74 – Statistic from Stephen Follows, 2017.
p74 – Data from Netflix on 2017 – A Year in Bingeing Press Release, Netflix, 2017, 2017.
p74 – Data from Technology for Publishing, 2016.
p74 – Data from Merch Dope, 2018.
p74 – Statistic from Inc., 2017.
p74 – Data from UNESCO, 2019.
p81 – Fact from Red Crow Marketing, 2015.

Macmillan Education Limited
4 Crinan Street
London N1 9XW

Companies and representatives throughout the world

Level 4 Student's Book ISBN 978-1-380-02032-1
Level 4 Student's Book Pack ISBN 978-1-380-02047-5

Text © Catherine McBeth 2019
Additional material by Laura Clyde

Design and illustration © Macmillan Education Limited 2019

The author has asserted their right to be identified as the author of this work in accordance with the Copyright, Designs and Patents Act 1988.

This edition published 2019
First edition entitled *Pulse* published 2014 by Macmillan Education Limited

All rights reserved. No part of this publication may be reproduced, stored in a retrieval system, or transmitted in any form or by any means, electronic, mechanical, photocopying, recording, or otherwise, without the prior written permission of the publishers.

Original design by Andrew Oliver
This edition design and page make-up by emc design
Illustrated by Mark Draisey pp.12; Arpad Olbey (Beehive Illustration) p.40-41; Nathalie Ortega (Beehive Illustration) pp.24, 62, 121
Cover design by Andrew Magee Design Limited
Cover illustration/photographs by Corbis; Flickr RF; Getty Images/ iStockphoto; Getty Images/Radius Images; Westend61.
Picture research by Julie-anne Wilce and Penelope Bowden

The author would like to express her gratitude to all the team at Macmillan for their support and enthusiasm.

The publishers would like to thank the following teachers for their contribution to the Project:
Alexia Vidal Seguí, Col·legi Sant Ferran, Barcelona; Amaya Eizaguirre Bolumburu, IES Lauiazeta BHI, San Sebastián – Donostia, Gipuzkoa; Anna Martín Rauret, Escola Isabel de Villena, Esplugues de Llobregat, Barcelona; Aurora Hernández Martínez, Institut La Mallola, Esplugues de Llobregat, Barcelona; Beatriz Sayalero Martín, IES Gran Capitán, Madrid; Cristina Ceide Ramírez, Institut Ítaca, Sant Boi de Llobregat, Barcelona; Esther Valbuena Ibáñez, Colegio Hijas de la Caridad. Nuestra Señora de Begoña, Bilbao, Bizkaia; Eva Farreny Mata, Col·legi Jesús María Claudina Thévenet, Barcelona; Julio César Fernández García, IES Galileo Galilei, Navia, Asturias; M.ª Ángeles Jiménez Fernández, Institut Centre d'Alt Rendiment, Sant Cugat del Vallés, Barcelona; M.ª Covadonga Gaitero Suarez, IES Parque de Lisboa, Alcorcón, Madrid; M.ª Purificación Pascual Mateos, Colegio Fundación Santamarca, Madrid; M.ª Teresa Gil Yanguas, IES Rafael Frühbeck de Burgos, Leganés, Madrid; Marta Ponti Alemany, Institut Menéndez y Pelayo, Barcelona; Olga Mata Burillo, Institut Les Corts, Barcelona; Rebeca Gorostieta López, C.P.E.I.P.S. SANTA MARIA H.L.B.H.I.P., Portugalete, Bizkaia; M.ª Jesús Páramo, Intitut Ernest Lluch, Barcelona; Yolanda Pérez Iborra, Colegio Calasancio, Alicante; Helena del Pico del Palacio, IES Julio Caro Baroja BHI, Algorta, Bizkaia.

The authors and publishers would like to thank the following for permission to reproduce their photographs: **Alamy Images** pp40,41, (mural), Alamy Images/Art Directors & TRIP p26(cards), Alamy Images/ Simon Belcher p6(t), Alamy Images/Cultura Creative (RF) p121(g), Alamy Images/Ian Dagnall p26(bottle), Alamy Images/Denkou Images p32, Alamy Images/Lev Dolgachov p9(b), Alamy Images/dpa picture alliance archive p119(b), Alamy Images/Leo Francini p4(br), Alamy Images/Fresh Start Images p78, Alamy Images/David J. Green p66(mr), Alamy Images/ Gennadiy Kravchenko p54(ml), Alamy Images/Peter Lane p119(a), Alamy Images/Thomas LENNE p83(c), Alamy Images/Nick Lylak p36(cl), Alamy Images/MBI p62(r), Alamy Images/Eetu Mustonen p10(t), Alamy Images/PhotoAlto pp94(ml), 123(l), Alamy Images/Pictorial Press Ltd p95, Alamy Images/Radius Images p18, Alamy Images/robertharding p4(mr), Alamy Images/Seaphotoart p6(b), Alamy Images/Shotshop GmbH p115(r), Alamy Images/shotstock p56(d), Alamy Images/Andrew Shurtleff p118(a,b), Alamy Images/Eric Simard p46(cl), Alamy Images/ Tetra Images p85, Alamy Images/Markus Thomenius p25, Alamy Images/ Alex White p56(a), Alamy Images/Maksym Yemelyanov p56(f), Alamy Images/Hongqi Zhang p98(l); **By kind permission of Eric Alper** p68; **BrandX** p121(a); **Photo courtesy of Broadreach** p30(t); **Glen Burrows & by kind permission of Katherine Mills** pp10, 11; **By kind permission of Children's Miracle Network Hospitals** p41; **By kind permission of EngineeringUK** pp50, 51; **Energy Tracker** p110(b); **Getty Images** p110(bl), Getty Images/Á© Hello Lovely/Corbis pp116(r), 122(l), Getty Images/Tony Anderson p44(t), Getty Images/AFP Contributor pp19(b), 89(1), Getty Images/Mahesh Balasubramanian/EyeEm p91, Getty Images/Thomas Barwick p48(l), Getty Images/Doug Berry p12(b), Getty Images/Bettmann p65(tr), Getty Images/Phil Boorman p93(l), Getty Images/John Burke p69(mr), Getty Images/d3sign p83(d), Getty Images/Caiaimage/Robert Daly p35(l), Getty Images/Steve Debenport p117, Getty Images/Caiaimage/Sam Edwards p116(l), Getty Images/ Caiaimage/Chris Ryan p89, Getty Images/Ken Chernus p29(br), Getty Images/Colin Anderson Productions Pty Ltd p49(tr,background), Getty Images/CSA Images p75r, Getty Images/Cultura RF p121(d), Getty Images/DanielPrudek p22(r), Getty Images/Artur Debat p29(tr), Getty Images/deepblue4you p9(t), Getty Images/DeepDesertPhoto p21,Getty Images/dreamnikon pp53, 89(4), Getty Images/EyeEm p7, Getty Images/ Sarah Fix p34(t), Getty Images/fotoVoyager 32(b), Getty Images/Tony C French pp80,81(background),Getty Images/gaffera p26(keys), Getty Images/Mark Garlick/Science Photo Library, p31(tl), Getty Images/ SEAN GLADWELL p93(r), Getty Images/Hero Images pp16(ml), 71, Getty Images/Billy Hustace p19(c), Getty Images/jlmatt p122(r), Getty Images/ JohnnyGreig p101, Getty Images/Johner Images pp9(m), 118(boy), Getty Images/Jose Luis Pelaez Inc p115(l), Getty Images/justinmedia p54(br), Getty Images/kana p79(drink), Getty Images/Stígur Már Karlsson/ Heimsmyndir p123(r), Getty Images/kate_sept2004 p35(l), Getty Images/ Howard Kingsnorth p4(tc), Getty Images/MarioGuti p79(billboard), Getty Images/Maskot p69(b), Getty Images/metamorworks p52(br), Getty Images/mgturner p83(f), Getty Images/Daniel Milchev p14(mr), Getty Images/mustafahacalaki p74(mr), Getty Images/Fabio Nodari p55, Getty Images/OJO Images p83(b), Getty Images/Ramiro Olaciregui p19(a), Getty Images/Opla p17(a), Getty Images/quavondo p43, Getty Images/Juan Manuel Rodriguez/EyeEm p86(r), Getty Images/ RUSSELLTATEdotCOM p59(b), Getty Images/RyanJLane pp52(ml), 89(10), Getty Images/MATJAZ SLANIC p83(a), Getty Images/Chad Slattery p83(e), Getty Images/Nuthawut Somsuk p34(b), Getty Images/ Karl Spencer p20, Getty Images/STOCK4B p44(tr), Getty Images/ StratosGiannikos p121(c), Getty Images/strmko p30(b), Getty Images/ Rudy Sulgan p35(r), Getty Images/Tetra Images p29(bm), Getty Images/ TimeStopper p60, Getty Images/Christine Wehrmeier p6(m), Getty Images/Westend61 p19(d), Getty Images/yangwenshuang p49(tr), Getty Images/Edward L. Zhao p8, Getty Images/Arman Zhenikeyev pp4(c), 89(7), Getty Images/Gale Zucker p108(br); **GLIMPSE** pp80,89(14); **iStock** p121(f); **L-Lingo** p110(a); **Mountain Rescue** p24(l); **By kind permission of National Citizen Service** p14; **Oxfam GB** p68(l); **PhotoDisc/** Getty Images pp59(t), 121(b); **Science Photo Library**/VICTOR DE SCHWANBERG p64; **Shutterstock.com** p28, Shutterstock.com/aapsky p103, Shutterstock.com/Rufat Bunyadzada p56(c), Shutterstock.com/ Film 4/Celador Films/Pathe International/Kobal p15, Shutterstock. com/ Mariusz S. Jurgielewicz p69(t), Shutterstock.com/Jane Kelly p56(e), Shutterstock.com/LightField Studios p58, Shutterstock.com/ Jay Maidment/Eon/Danjaq/Sony/Kobal p75(b), Shutterstock.com/ Marco's studio p121(cm), Shutterstock.com/Gino Santa Maria p19(t), Shutterstock.com/ Luciano Mortula - LGM p79(t), Shutterstock.com/ Orkhan Naghiyev p56(b), Shutterstock.com/Piotr Piatrouski p73, Shutterstock.com/View Apart 39(tr); **Macmillan Education Ltd** pp12(t), 16)t), 17, 22(tc), 26(tr), 26(sweets), 27, 32(t), 38, 42, 46(tr), 47, 52(tl),